Praise for *Stop Over-Thi*

"Preet is one of the best. He out and out gets it. He's truly passionate about helping Canadians handle their money wisely. As important, he has the knowledge and communication skills to do it."

—**David Chilton**, author of the bestselling books *The Wealthy Barber* and *The Wealthy Barber Returns*, and the new Dragon on CBC's *The Dragon's Den*

"We all know that despite our best-laid plans, crap happens! Preet wants you to know how to protect yourself so that when it does, you have options. This book has a simple, straightforward message about building a strong personal foundation instead of the 'sexy' investment stuff no one can ever put into practice because *they don't have the money* to take it to that next level. Five simple rules. That's all. Follow them."

—**Gail Vaz-Oxlade**, TV host and bestselling author of *Money Rules* and *Debt-Free Forever*

"Managing money isn't hard. But you can be confused, or paralyzed, by all the conflicting information. Preet Banerjee helps you sort through the spin and find the truth about keeping your finances on track. He acts as a trusted friend who talks in terms you can understand without talking down to you." —**Ellen Roseman**, personal finance columnist, *Toronto Star*

"Just the totally in-your-face talking-to that Canadians need to improve their financial health. Stop making excuses and read this no-nonsense book."

—**Rob Carrick**, personal finance columnist,
The Globe and Mail

"Banerjee focuses on five basic principles of personal finance that will benefit not just the average financial illiterate but even supposedly sophisticated investors who are guilty of 'over-thinking' their portfolios. In other words, when it comes to money, most of us need to learn to walk before trying to run."

—**Jonathan Chevreau**, editor of *MoneySense*
and author of *Findependence Day*

"[Contains] simple, straightforward advice that you can use immediately and will benefit you for a lifetime. Preet has extracted the complexity from finances, and we are left with a usable tome that can change lives. Well done, Preet."
—**Tom Hamza**, president,
Investor Education Fund

STOP OVER-THINKING YOUR MONEY!

PREET BANERJEE inspires others to become financially empowered with his unique ability to take the complexity out of money matters. He writes a personal finance column for *The Globe and Mail* and is the money expert for the W Network, the host of *Million Dollar Neighborhood* on the Oprah Winfrey Network (Canada), and a financial panelist on CBC's *The National with Peter Mansbridge*.

His blog, WhereDoesAllMyMoneyGo.com, was voted Canada's best investing blog, and Advisor.ca named him one of Canada's Top 10 Financial Visionaries. Banerjee also hosts a podcast on iTunes, "Mostly Money, Mostly Canadian," which is one of the highest rated podcasts in Canada for business and investing.

He is a fellow of the Canadian Securities Institute (FCSI) and also holds the designations of derivatives market specialist (DMS) and finance management advisor (FMA). He was awarded first place in the 2012 Portfolio Management Association of Canada's Excellence in Investment Journalism Awards.

His website is located at www.preetbanerjee.com. Follow him on Twitter @preetbanerjee.

PREET BANERJEE

STOP OVER-THINKING YOUR MONEY!

THE FIVE SIMPLE RULES OF FINANCIAL SUCCESS

PORTFOLIO
PENGUIN

PORTFOLIO PENGUIN
an imprint of Penguin Canada Books Inc., a Penguin Random House Company

Published by the Penguin Group
Penguin Canada Books Inc.
320 Front Street West, Suite 1400, Toronto, Ontario M5V 3B6, Canada

Penguin Group (USA) LLC, 375 Hudson Street, New York, New York 10014, U.S.A.
Penguin Books Ltd, 80 Strand, London WC2R 0RL, England
Penguin Ireland, 25 St Stephen's Green, Dublin 2, Ireland (a division of Penguin Books Ltd)
Penguin Group (Australia), 707 Collins Street, Melbourne, Victoria 3008, Australia
   (a division of Pearson Australia Group Pty Ltd)
Penguin Books India Pvt Ltd, 11 Community Centre, Panchsheel Park, New Delhi – 110 017, India
Penguin Group (NZ), 67 Apollo Drive, Rosedale, Auckland 0632, New Zealand
   (a division of Pearson New Zealand Ltd)
Penguin Books (South Africa) (Pty) Ltd, 24 Sturdee Avenue, Rosebank,
   Johannesburg 2196, South Africa

Penguin Books Ltd, Registered Offices: 80 Strand, London WC2R 0RL, England

First published 2014

3 4 5 6 7 8 9 10 (RRD)

Manufactured in the U.S.A.

LIBRARY AND ARCHIVES CANADA CATALOGUING IN PUBLICATION

Banerjee, Preet, author
Stop over-thinking your money! : the five simple rules of financial success / Preet Banerjee.

ISBN 978-0-14-318351-8 (pbk.)

1. Finance, Personal. I. Title.

HG179.B338 2014   332.024   C2012-906281-2

Visit the Penguin Canada website at www.penguin.ca

Special and corporate bulk purchase rates available; please see
www.penguin.ca/corporatesales or call 1-800-810-3104.

THIS BOOK IS DEDICATED TO MY WONDERFUL MOTHER,
PARTLY BECAUSE SHE THREATENED ME,
BUT MOSTLY BECAUSE SHE IS THE WARMEST,
MOST LOVING PERSON I KNOW. I LOVE YOU, MOM!

CONTENTS

INTRODUCTION

There are thousands of books on personal finance, investing, debt management, and everything else there is to know about money. You would have to become a full-time reader in order to get through even half of it in your lifetime. The good news is that you don't have to do that to be financially successful. Not even close.

I want this book to make it clear that in order to be in control of your money, you just have to get the fundamentals down pat. And forget what you think you know about the fundamentals, or even what those fundamentals are. Let's start with a tabula rasa, a blank slate, and go from there.

Here are the five simple rules for personal financial success:

1. Disaster-proof your life.
2. Spend less than you earn.

3. Aggressively pay down high-interest debt.
4. Read the fine print.
5. Delay consumption.

I guarantee that if you can follow these five rules, you'll be better off than most people.

Cue the whimpering party favour that sounds like a dying duck. Yep! On practically the first page I've given you all you need to know about the fundamentals of being financially successful. Maybe it seems like a letdown. Maybe you were expecting some secret, magic-bullet solution to all your financial problems and questions. That doesn't exist. The truth is, you've either been over-thinking your money, or you haven't been thinking about it at all. And it's time for that to stop.

Consider the goal of leading a healthier life. We know that if we eat better and work out regularly, we'll be in better shape. We also know that people who use personal trainers often get fantastic results. But it's not because the personal trainer shows you a fancy new way to do a sit-up; the trainer just makes you do the sit-up. When you make an appointment to meet your trainer at the gym, you're more likely to show up than if you were going to work out by yourself. And he or she kicks your butt when you get there. If you can do 10 push-ups without breaking a sweat, that's not a workout, that's a warm-up. Your trainer won't let you stop until you're sweating, and you know that because of that discipline, you are going to see results.

But I have good news.

Getting physically fit is much harder than getting financially fit. Physically, you have to bust your ass forever to see continual improvement. Very few people have the commitment to do that. Financially, you need that kind of discipline for only a short time, because once you get started down the right path, it gets easier. You'll get to a point where you have more money left over at the end of the month, and then you can put it away to grow in a savings account or investment portfolio. All things being equal, your income is rising as well, so you can ease off on the discipline. Eventually, you'll get to a point where your financial situation improves without your having to make a huge effort. It's as if your financial muscles are growing bigger and bigger and you're not even going to the gym anymore.

That's it. That might sound ridiculously simple, but it works.

Many people are convinced that they need to get everything figured out before they can start overhauling their finances. They think they need a perfect plan. But making a perfect plan is so daunting a task that they never make a start. The difference between a good plan and a perfect plan is like the difference between an

A and an A+. Considering most people are somewhere near a C−, an easy A seems like a much better goal than a hard-to-get A+. This book is going to show you how to get that easy A. If you want that A+, then, as I've already said, there are thousands of books out there from which to start your long campaign.

When I was a financial advisor, I met people with different "money personalities." The people who had lots of money blew me away with how poorly they understood the complexities of investments (which are not as important as most people think). Meanwhile, the people who could rattle off the price of gold, or give me the price history of BlackBerry's stock for the last five years generally were not the ones with loads of cash. In the beginning, building up lots of money depends more on putting money away than making money grow because of smart investing decisions. Put $200 per month into a high-interest savings account that pays a measly 1.5% and you'll have almost $26,000 after 10 years. Invest only $100 per month and to get a comparable outcome, just shy of $26,000, you'll need an annualized return of more than 14% per year on your portfolio. (The long-term return for stock market investments is about 6–8%, so, in other words, that result is extremely unlikely.) Anything that has the potential to earn that much also has a very high chance of losing a lot, too. We'll go over the basics of risk and return later, because a little risk is okay for some people, but the point is that how much you save is far more important than trying to beat the market. You'll also note that you can control one of these options (how much you save), but you have almost no control over the other (market performance).

Think about that: when you are starting out, how much you save is far more important that trying to outperform the market.

Saving is simple. You either do it or you don't. You don't need to read a textbook that tells you what saving money is: it's just putting money away. Investing, on the other hand, is infinitely more complex. Professional investors who manage billions of dollars are always assimilating new information. And they already know a lot. They've already spent hundreds or thousands of hours studying to get licensed, and even after that, they study more. They're immersed in the business: it's what they do for a living. And most don't beat the market.

This is a perfect example of the way most people complicate money unnecessarily. And it explains why my most successful clients were the ones who just did the simple things well. You don't have to understand what the talking heads are saying on the business news to be financially successful. You just have to get the basics right.

I've just used saving and investing as my first example of over-thinking. I chose this topic partly because it's sexier than life insurance (well, the investing part, that is). People who consider themselves to be well-informed about money are generally the ones who watch the business news, read the business section of the newspaper, and follow a few financial blogs. All three of those media put little emphasis on financial planning and lots of emphasis on investing. It has been burned into our heads that investing prowess is equated with good money management.

I call bullshit.

The truth is that investing is pretty close to the last thing you need to worry about. Some of you may have noticed that when I listed the five rules for financial success, investing wasn't even mentioned. That was no mistake.

Rule number one is to disaster-proof your life. This is simply because you may be hit by a bus tomorrow. Or lose your job. Or discover a mole that turns out to be cancer. Your personal financial situation could be completely upended in a flash. The risks are even greater when you are younger because you haven't had time to build up assets you can liquidate.

Planning for retirement is a multi-decade endeavour. You have time to figure that out. However, you don't have all the time in the world to figure out your insurance. As a former colleague of mine used to say, "If you know the day you are going to die, give me a call, and I'll pop over the night before and set up your insurance policy." The absurdity of that proposition is clear. Ditto for disability insurance, in case you don't lose your life, but instead lose the ability to work for a living. According to insurance company Great-West Life, one in three people become disabled for 90 days or more before age 65, and of those people, their average length of disability is 2.9 years. If you found out today that you wouldn't have income from employment for three years, how long could you last financially?

The next two rules—spend less than you earn and aggressively pay down high-interest debt—are related. Debt is built up because you spend money you don't have (yet). Anyone who has built up significant debt knows that it handcuffs you. Many people reach a state of equilibrium in which they make the odd lump-sum payment against their credit card balances and yet never quite pay it off. They feel as though they never get ahead. They make hundreds, even thousands of dollars of payments that could be used towards so many other things: savings, retirement, vacations, emergency funds—you name it.

The fourth rule is to read the fine print. Most people are guilty of not even reading the large print, but the small type is where you generally find the clauses that come back to bite you later. I know a lot of people skip it, either because they don't want to take up a salesperson's time, or because there is too much to read, and those are silly reasons. Never sign anything at your front door the first time you meet someone, and never sign anything you don't understand. Pay special attention to what happens when you want to cancel or back out of a contract.

The fifth rule—delay consumption—is probably the hardest to implement in the beginning, but it becomes self-reinforcing over time. We've all sometimes been tempted to "keep up with the Joneses," as the saying goes, but we shouldn't, because they're headed for a cliff.

If you've ever gone to a big-box electronics store and admired the rows of high-definition televisions on display, then you have seen a perfect example of the Jones phenomenon in action. When you see two TVs of the same size side by side, but at vastly different prices, the one with the higher price may look sharper, be slightly thinner, have better contrast or more vivid colour. There is a tendency to gravitate to the higher-priced model because, when looked at that way, the difference between it and the cheaper, less expensive model can be very noticeable. But if you take the cheaper model home, where there is no other TV beside it to compare it with, you won't notice a thing that gets in the way of enjoying your TV shows and movies. When we compare, we compete. And our survival-of-the-fittest mentality means we try to win.

But delayed consumption is about more than just TVs. The big-ticket items, such as houses and cars, are where we can really draw the line between needs and wants, and between financial success and financial strife.

So that's it. Five simple rules. So far, I haven't thrown out any acronyms, formulas, complex calculations, or strategies. Nor have I said you need to cut out your daily takeout coffee or any of your other minor vices. It's possible to be financially prudent and still have fun. If you can run a surplus, and put that surplus to good use, drink all the lattes you want. What would be the point of trying to amass any kind of wealth if not to spend it eventually? And how likely is someone to stick to a plan if it's so difficult that it's impossible to stay motivated? (Having said that, some people might choose to give up takeout coffees because they would rather spend some money on other vices. Not everyone likes caffeine as much as I do.)

What follows is a blueprint showing how you can score an easy A with your personal finances. As I said before, if you want that hard-to-get A+, by no means should you stop at reading only this book. I'll cover the basics of how to invest prudently, but I won't drill down on whether you would be better off using index mutual funds versus exchange-traded index funds after factoring in the commissions versus management expense ratios at various portfolio sizes. That would be like talking about how a race-car driver can use both feet to operate all three pedals simultaneously when you don't even know how to drive stick or what a clutch is. That's an A+ discussion. It's certainly worth exploring, but not until later.

An A+ is better than an A, but an easy A is way better than the C– most people are currently scoring.

When you've finished this book, feel free to ask me anything on Twitter at @preetbanerjee. I'd love to hear from you and show you how to graduate from an A to an A+.

PART 1

THE FIVE RULES

As you read through Part 1, I want you to consciously remember that most of what you will read won't be earth-shattering. It won't be hard to understand, but it will be hard to execute. Keep in mind the analogy with physical fitness. We know we have to work out and eat better to improve our health. There's nothing complex about that. Honestly, if you do anything in the gym for 45 minutes, three times per week, and avoid eating junk, you'll see results over time. But getting to the gym and resisting unhealthy treats are incredibly hard challenges for most of us.

It's not entirely clear what the money-management equivalents to exercise and a proper diet are. That's what we're starting with. After I show you how to do the financial equivalent of a basic sit-up and what foods to eat or avoid, the rest is up to you.

CHAPTER ONE

RULE 1: DISASTER-PROOF YOUR LIFE

"Can you look at my investments?"

That's a question I get asked a lot. And if it's not that specific one, it generally still has to do with investing. Some people equate financial advice with the stock market and nothing more. It's hard to blame them. Any business program on TV, business section in the newspaper, or segment devoted to economic issues on the radio has a ratio of investing news to personal finance information of about 20:1.

Investing is just one of many factors that affect your personal finances. And it takes a long time to get acclimated to the lingo and to learn the ropes. It also takes a long time to accumulate a sizeable portfolio, to the tune of decades. Retirement, which is a concept that probably should be retired itself, is often associated with stopping work at age 65. So if you want to have a proper, traditional retirement, you're going to have to sock money away for a long time.

Without downplaying the importance of saving and investing, it's worth emphasizing that there are a lot of things that can happen to you before your ideal retirement age that could derail those plans. You might die before 65. You might lose your job. You might get sick to the point where you can't work. You might be injured and become disabled. You might have any number of incredibly expensive emergencies crop up.

Any of these developments can be fatal to your long-term retirement savings plan because they jeopardize your ability to save for your retirement portfolio. But it's not only your retirement that is at stake. Your way of life is too. Your ability to keep your home, your car, and to put food on the table is also at risk. Any one of these disasters can leave a family destitute.

Here are the basic ways you can protect yourself against various disasters:

- disability insurance in the event that you become disabled (caused either by injury or ill health);
- life insurance, which protects your family's lifestyle in the event of your death;
- an emergency fund for loss of employment or unexpected emergencies;

- wills and powers of attorney to help
  communicate your wishes to others if you can't
  do so yourself.

Let's look at each of them in turn.

DISABILITY INSURANCE

Disability insurance pays you a monthly benefit in the event that you lose the ability to work. You pay a premium (the cost of the policy) and if you become disabled, you are then entitled to monthly benefits for a specified period of time, known as the "benefit period." The monthly benefit usually does not start to be paid until a few months after you become disabled. This delay—normally 90 days—is known as the "elimination period."

For example, let's say you are a graphic designer earning $60,000 per year. On the way home from work one day, you are involved in a car accident and become disabled. You are no longer physically able to work due to the injury sustained in the crash. After the elimination period (let's say it's the standard 90 days), you start to get a monthly benefit, which replaces part of your take-home pay, from your disability insurance provider.

The disability might also be caused by a health condition. For example, you could be diagnosed with multiple sclerosis and the symptoms could prevent you from working.

Some people have disability insurance as part of a benefits package at work, but most don't realize how valuable it is. Unless they have to make a claim.

I recently met two men, both of whom were disabled. One had benefits at work that provided disability insurance coverage, and the other didn't. The person with coverage has no debt outside his mortgage, and his wife currently is a stay-at-home mom to their two children. They are in no danger of losing their home. The person who didn't have coverage lives with his wife on $1,600 per month provided by government benefits. After paying rent, utilities, and groceries, they have maybe $200 per month for everything else. Their credit cards are maxed.

Both these men will tell you that disability insurance is a necessity, not an option.

You insure your house and car. You might even insure every electronic gadget you buy with an extended warranty (which could be a big mistake, by the way). But what about your single biggest asset: the ability to earn an income for the rest of your life?

Let's put it into context. Assume that as a university graduate, you start your working career earning

$45,000 per year. Assuming raises and promotions over time, your salary grows by perhaps 4% per year on average. Over a 40-year career, that translates into total earnings of more than $4.25 million. Over that time, part of your take-home pay is slowly converted into tangible assets and investments, but while you are younger, your future earnings are among the most important aspects of your financial well-being. That potential is your biggest asset, even though it won't show up on a balance sheet for years. How well protected is that asset?

Life insurance can be structured to provide your family with an ongoing means to sustain, after your death, the lifestyle you have created in your lifetime. But what happens if you don't die from an accident or health ailment, but suffer an injury serious enough to keep you from working? What if you become disabled for an extended period? It's a sad truth that sometimes people would have been better off financially if they had died, instead of surviving with some form of physical handicap, simply because they didn't take the time to ensure they had proper disability insurance coverage. It's a morbid thought, but think about it: the mortgage still needs to be paid; you may want to pay for special devices or services to assist with coping with your disability. The accident or illness could lead to your having to downsize your lifestyle. You might have to move to a smaller house, cut out some luxuries, and so on.

As I mentioned in the introduction, Great-West Life reports that one in three people will become disabled for longer than 90 days before age 65, and the average length of disability that lasts more than 90 days is 2.9 years.

If you have a benefits plan at work, then you'll want to find out what your coverage is exactly. Some plans provide a benefit for only five years, while others provide a benefit until you are 65. The percentage of income replaced also varies. If you've lost your employee handbook, call your HR department and get to know the details of your disability coverage. Some people discover that it needs to be topped up with a private plan, one that covers the difference between what you're earning at work and what you would ideally like to have as replacement income.

If you are self-employed, or don't have a benefits plan, run, don't walk, to get a disability quote from an insurance agent. Be prepared for the sticker shock, because policies can sometimes run to more than $100 per month—but remember, disability coverage may be your most expensive insurance policy because the asset you are protecting is potentially your biggest.

As a real-world example, my disability insurance policy will provide $2,500 per month should I become disabled, and it will be paid to me until I turn 65. I'm currently 35, and my annual cost is $820 per year. It would've been $73.81 per month, but you save money by paying annually instead of monthly. In my case, I save $65.72 a year by making a single annual payment.

There are many factors that affect the premium of a disability insurance policy. Someone who works in construction is more likely to get hurt than I am, because most of the time I work at a desk or in front of a camera, where mishaps are relatively rare. It might cost the construction worker more for the same policy for this reason. You can also choose a shorter benefit period, instead of "to age 65," which is what I selected. For example, you could pick a benefit period of five years. If I became disabled today I would receive $2,500 per month for 30 years (and the amount would actually increase over time with inflation, because I chose that option). When you factor in the gradual increases in the benefit, the value of the policy could add up to more than $1.2 million. If I chose only a five-year benefit period, the total paid to me would be just over $150,000. Because the insurance company would be on the hook for less, the premiums would be cheaper.

You can lower your benefit amount or increase your elimination period as well. There are many options you can adjust (or, realistically, have an insurance agent adjust to see what works best for your budget if you're tight on cash flow). If you had to choose between cutting the length of the benefit period and decreasing the benefit amount, it might be wise to start with decreasing the benefit amount, but keep the coverage to age 65.

There are also various bells and whistles you can add to the policy. What we might normally call "extra options" are referred to as "riders" in the world of insurance. An example would be a rider that increases your benefit with inflation. Since that means a larger overall benefit to you if you make a claim, it increases the premium you pay for the policy.

There are different types of disability-insurance plans offered by the major insurance companies, all with different features and benefits. Because it is so important, I highly recommend that you take the time to sit down with an agent to sort it all out. You don't want to make mistakes with any financial decisions, but with something as important as disability insurance, you really need to find an experienced agent who is willing to take the time to explain your options. Don't delay in making an appointment, but don't rush through the process once you've started it. Make sure you're comfortable with the decision you make.

I can't stress this enough: run, don't walk, to make an appointment with someone to talk about this if you don't have coverage. You can't get it after you become disabled, and if you do become disabled without coverage, it's almost guaranteed that you will be poor forever.

I'm serious! Put down the book and send an email, or make a phone call now! Arrange to talk to at least two different insurance agents from different companies and get the ball rolling. The application process can take a few weeks and you don't have to pay until a contract with your final cost is in your hands. You can back out anytime.

If you're thinking, "I'll get to it," either you've missed the point or you think you're invincible. There are five simple rules for financial success. Five. You don't get to pick and choose which ones to follow. You need to follow them all.

LIFE INSURANCE

Life insurance pays what is called a "death benefit," which is just a lump sum of money, to a beneficiary in case you die. You pay a "premium" (the cost of the policy), and when you die, a designated person receives a cheque for the benefit amount. It's pretty straightforward in the general sense. But there are a few nuances you need to become familiar with.

If you have dependants (people who rely on you to support their lifestyle), the loss of your income can change their lives. Many people buy life insurance to minimize or eliminate any financial changes in the lifestyle of their loved ones. You might want to ensure that your dependants can remain in the family home, that the children can be supported until they are independent, and to make sure there is no financial hardship on top of the emotional hardship brought about by your passing.

Most people seem to know that they need life insurance if they have dependants, and they seem to know it if they have children, but too many of those same people don't actually have life insurance, or they have the incorrect amount, or think their group benefits plan at work is all they need (it may or may not be).

This is a perfect example of people knowing what they have to do but not doing it. Some of you are reading this right now, know you need life insurance, and still don't have any. What exactly are you waiting for? Actually take a minute and decide for yourself why you are waiting. Again, seriously, put down the book for a minute and take the time to think about it. You need to make this a priority. Not, "I'll get this done this year," but, "I'll be sitting in front of an insurance agent by next week."

You might be thinking that the chances of your dying are low because you're relatively young. Well, the good news is that life insurance premiums reflect your likely lifespan. I just bought a new life insurance policy for $250,000, and, as a 35-year-old, it's costing me less than $16 per month ($187.50 per year to be exact).

I've shared a short story about life insurance in Chapter 8. I recommend that you read that story before you meet with an insurance agent, just to bring you up to speed. The rest of this section deals with some other important nuances you might not otherwise have considered.

When Is the Underwriting Performed?

"Underwriting" is the process of determining if a person is eligible for an insurance product and how much risk the insurance company feels it is taking by offering this person an insurance policy. This assessed risk is used to establish just how much a particular insurance policy will cost. There is a difference between insurance policies that have the underwriting performed at the time of claim (which, for life insurance, means when you die) versus underwriting that is performed at the time of application.

I hope the concept of figuring out whether someone qualified for life insurance after they are no longer living strikes you as odd. On occasion, it has led people to pay life insurance premiums for years only to discover that, when they die, their beneficiaries do not get the lump-sum death benefit that was expected.

On the other hand, underwriting at the time the application is made, which can involve a nurse coming to your house to take your blood pressure and collect a urine sample before you get a policy in your hands, leads to a much more robust life insurance policy. Death for any reason, except suicide, usually triggers payment of the benefit from day one of the policy coming into force. After 2 years of the policy being in force, your beneficiaries could still receive the death benefit even if you committed suicide (as long as it wasn't a part of some insurance-fraud scheme).

Underwriting at application can seem like a hassle. There can be lots of questions, some of which might make you uncomfortable, and some people just hate needles. There can be a tedious follow-up by the insurance company with your family doctor if the company feels anything needs to be checked out further. The company may even insist on waiting for the results of your annual physical. But once it's done, it's done, and you know you have robust coverage when underwriting is performed at the time of application.

Contrast this with an insurance policy based on the answers to a few yes-or-no questions over the phone or on a simple one-page form. That basic test is just a screen to see if you are terminally ill right now (and would be denied coverage right away). The actual underwriting hasn't been done and won't be done until you make a claim (die). That's the worst time to find out that you didn't actually qualify for the coverage (or rather, for whomever is making the claim on your behalf to make that discovery). The company might refund the premiums paid, but that sum might be a drop in the bucket compared to the insurance benefit you were counting on.

In short, it's worth the hassle and discomfort to get the full underwriting done at the time you make the application. You can do this by getting a private life insurance policy through an insurance agent. One other advantage of private insurance is that if you are healthier than average, your premiums will be lower to reflect the reduced risk of your dying anytime soon. The flip side of that coin is that, if you are less healthy than average, your premiums will be higher than average to reflect the increased risk that you will die sooner rather than later.

If you have life insurance provided through your group benefits plan at work, it is imperative to understand your coverage. That means you actually have to read your group benefits handbook. The same holds true for your disability insurance provided through work. I'll go into more detail on reading the fine print in Chapter 4. There, I'll include a real-world example of an individual who had both a private life insurance policy and a creditor-based life insurance policy (sold with his mortgage by the lender). The person died and the private policy paid the death benefit in two weeks, while the creditor-based policy denied the claim. Imagine if that family only had the latter policy!

Term Life Insurance versus Permanent Insurance

When they talk about life insurance, I doubt that most educators lead off with the issue of when the underwriting is performed. They might start with the difference between temporary insurance and permanent insurance. But I tackled the underwriting issue first because there are many people who think they obtained full coverage when they ticked a box on their mortgage application, indicating that they had applied for mortgage life insurance. Yes, you might have life insurance of some kind, but if that policy doesn't actually pay out when you die, that's a big problem.

Having got that off my chest, let's discuss the two main types of life insurance. Term life insurance is sometimes referred to as "temporary" life insurance. It is commonly described as coverage you rent for a while, until you no longer need it. That time could be when you've built up an estate large enough that you are effectively self-insured. If you are 65, have all your ducks in a row, and have a net worth of $1 million, you might not need that life insurance policy worth a few hundred thousand dollars, at least not for the original purpose, which was to make sure your family's lifestyle was not devastated if you died when you were younger. They might have experienced considerable hardship then, when you were a young family with no assets, lots of debt, and a baby or two. Your situation changes as you grow up and grow old.

Life insurance premiums are directly related to your risk of dying. If you're 20, you're less likely to die than someone who is 50, for obvious reasons. When you're 80, your chances of dying are high enough that trying to get a new life insurance policy would be cost-prohibitive. It follows that as you get older and your risk of dying increases, the premiums on a life insurance policy get bigger.

A term life insurance policy sets the premium to a constant level for the duration of the term, which could be 5 years, 10 years, or longer. So if you have a 10-year term life insurance policy for $250,000 of coverage, you might get quoted a cost of $16.88 per month (that's the exact figure I was quoted as a 35-year-old). That $16.88 monthly premium will stay the same for the next 10 years. You can save money by paying annually instead of monthly: my annual premium is $187.50 (a 7% saving). When I'm 45, the premium increases to $1,052.50 per year for the next 10 years until I turn

55. At that point, it would be scheduled to increase to $2,337.50 per year for the next 10 years. And so on. (If those increases in the premiums scare you, keep reading this section for a trick to dramatically reduce the costs over time.) If I ever choose to stop paying my premiums, the policy will lapse. I owe the insurance company nothing, and it is no longer on the hook to pay my beneficiary a death benefit. That's why it's called "temporary" insurance.

Permanent insurance is designed to address the increase in the cost of insurance as you get older, assuming you continue to need the coverage when you are very old. Permanent insurance is priced so that you pay the same premium your whole life, which is where the name "whole life insurance" comes from. That means it's much more expensive than term insurance at the beginning of the policy, but much cheaper at the end. Really what is happening is that the extra cost up front (compared to a term life policy purchased at the same age) is set aside into a reserve account. Later, when the premiums of a whole life policy are lower than term life, that shortfall is covered by tapping into the built-up reserve. The result is that you overpay for insurance early in the policy and underpay for it later, but your premiums stay the same your whole life.

For example, my 10-year term life policy with

$250,000 in coverage costs me $187.50 per year for the next 10 years. The same $250,000 of whole life coverage would be close to $1,500 per year forever. That's almost 10 times as expensive to start. If I kept my 10-year term life policy and just let it renew at the higher premiums every 10 years, by the time I was 75 my annual premium would be $20,155. Even if I re-qualify as healthy (to get a better rate) when I'm 75, a 10-year term life insurance policy for $250,000 at that time might be $8,072.50 per year. The whole life policy would be looking incredibly cheap at that time, but that assumes I kept paying the premiums since I was 35.

But why would I need $250,000 when I die, if I live to be 75? Presumably, I will have saved some money over my career. If I have had kids, they had better be out of the house and self-sufficient. In fact, I would hope to have a sizeable estate, enough that I could leave a small inheritance to my spouse, children, or their children. So there are reasons to think that permanent insurance is unnecessary for many people. There are exceptions, of course.

Term life insurance is much more affordable than permanent insurance when you are younger, which is the time you need life insurance the most. As you get older, and with planning and good fortune, build up your estate, your need for life insurance decreases. This is why most people are better off with term life insurance. While the unit cost of insurance increases over time, the number of units you need decreases as your assets grow. If you were the family breadwinner, with a stay-at-home spouse and two young children, your death would be devastating, emotionally and financially. If you earned $50,000 per year, you might want 15 years of income replacement ($50,000 × 15 = $750,000) so that your family could retain the same home and lifestyle they would have if you were alive. That might be enough to see the children move out, and for your spouse to establish a career and become self-sufficient. If you're 55, have a spouse who earns an income, the kids have moved out, and you're mortgage-free, there may not be a need for income replacement at all.

To determine how much insurance you should have, you need what is known as an "insurance needs analysis." This is a quick exercise that helps you to estimate your true insurance requirement. There are some simple online calculators you can try, but it's best to walk through it with an experienced agent.

See Chapter 8, where I explain the differences between term and whole life insurance in greater detail. That chapter concludes with a crude insurance needs analysis. After reading it, you'll be more up-to-speed when meeting with an insurance agent to discuss your options, and ready to go through a formal insurance needs analysis.

Already Have Life Insurance? Here's How to Save Big Bucks!

They say there are only two certainties in life: death and taxes. But a third could be rising life insurance premiums. But while life insurance is a necessity for most, there are ways to reduce your lifetime costs significantly. For many it could add up to tens of thousands of dollars.

As you know, the cost of life insurance goes up the older you are. It's also more expensive the less healthy you are. And actuaries (the people who determine what the premiums will ultimately be, based on mortality statistics, interest rates, and other factors) also know that if you qualify as healthy today, there is a chance that you will become unhealthy tomorrow.

Glenn Cooke, president of LifeInsuranceCanada. com, provided me with some real-life quotes to help demonstrate how this can affect the cost of your insurance.

For example, if you were a 40-year-old, non-smoking male in good health, and you wanted $500,000 of term life insurance coverage, one company quoted a monthly premium of $30.78 for a policy with a

10-year term. After the term is up, you can automatically renew, but the monthly premium increases to $231.75. Contrast this to the same coverage applied for today by a 50-year-old man: if he qualifies as healthy, his premium is only $71.42 per month.

According to Cooke, the reason for the difference is that the insurance companies use two different sets of mortality tables when pricing life policies. A "select" mortality table factors in your specific level of health, which is obtained after taking a medical assessment upon application for the policy. So the company knows exactly how healthy you are when the policy takes effect. The select mortality table is used only to price the insurance for the first term.

For every successive term, the policy is priced using what is called the "ultimate" mortality table. These are the statistics for the general population, which do not differentiate based on level of health. So the sample the table is based on includes unhealthy people who have a greater chance of dying sooner than their healthier counterparts, and who potentially would collect a large insurance benefit after having paid premiums for just a short while. The increased likelihood of large payouts gets factored in to the price, which means it goes up.

However, if you can still qualify as healthy, you can get a new policy at a lower rate and save big bucks.

(Remember never to cancel a policy until you have a new one in its place.) On the other hand, if you take a new medical assessment and find out that you have become uninsurable or otherwise unhealthy, you can take the opportunity to talk to your insurance advisor about converting the existing policy to a permanent one. Cooke says the ability to convert a policy is an important feature to look for. While a term life policy might not be the right solution for everyone, understanding how policies are priced over time can save you a lot of money.

Table 1.1 shows the premiums that might be paid by a healthy, non-smoking male with a term life insurance policy valued at $500,000 on a 10-year term, first, if the policy is renewed automatically, and second, if he re-qualifies as healthy each time the policy comes

Table 1.1: Term Life Insurance: The difference between automatic renewal and re-qualifying as healthy*

Age	Monthly Premium if Renewed Automatically	Monthly Premium if Re-qualified as Healthy
25–34	$27.90	$26.10
35–44	$58.95	$25.56
45–54	$122.85	$47.12
55–64	$304.65	$131.13

* Quotes provided by Glenn Cooke, life insurance broker and president of LifeInsuranceCanada.com

up for renewal. If the individual in this example renews his policy until age 65, his total premiums paid are $61,722.00. If he re-qualifies as healthy every 10 years until age 65, his total premiums are $27,589.20. The total amount saved by the individual who re-qualifies as healthy is $34,132.80.

AN EMERGENCY FUND

Emergencies happen all the time. An unexpected car repair, a flood in the basement, a cellphone bill with big roaming charges you didn't expect, a leaking roof, you name it. Some people call these unexpected events "life." And they really do happen more often than we expect. All of a sudden, if only temporarily, your income can't cover your expenses. But I've just described the expense side of that equation. There is also the income side to look at. Namely, losing your job.

The problem is still the same. You can temporarily be forced into a deficit situation where your expenses are greater than your income. This is the rainy day people have in mind when they're thinking of saving. The solution to either kind of emergency is to have an emergency fund. This is simply money kept in an easily accessible location that can be drawn upon on a rainy day.

I know what some readers are thinking. Do you create an emergency fund if you have lots of debt, especially high-interest debt, the kind charged by credit card companies? I'll get to that.

How big should your emergency fund be? Depending on who you talk to, the general rule of thumb is to hold anywhere from 3 months' worth of *expenses* to 12 months' worth of *income* in your emergency fund. Twelve months' worth of income might add up to more than $100,000 for some households. I can't imagine putting that much money aside into a high-interest savings account as a safety net, especially if you have a balance on your mortgage or credit cards. Just think how much faster your mortgage could be paid off with a lump-sum payment that big!

For that same household, 3 months' worth of expenses might be $10,000 or less. That's generally going to be plenty for most people, especially if you are doing all the other things you are supposed to be doing (insurance, investing, etc.). For example, if you contribute regularly to a retirement savings plan and you run into an emergency, isn't the logical solution to take some of those savings to meet the immediate need? Experts will tell you that it's a no-no to draw upon retirement savings for any reason other than retirement, but, in reality, that's exactly what most people would do.

Many people count their tax-free savings accounts (TFSAs), registered retirement savings plans (RRSPs), home equity, other investment accounts, and unused lines of credit as emergency reserves. Lines of credit may or may not be available when you need them, but the other sources are perfectly valid. That being the case, as you get closer to retirement, your need for an emergency reserve funded by a high-interest savings account decreases, because your assets have (or should have) increased.

Unless it causes you to lose sleep at night (in which case, you might want to set aside more), 3 months' worth of expenses kept in a high-interest savings account is more than enough for an emergency reserve. It should be in either a simple savings account or a cashable (which means you can access it at any time) guaranteed income certificate (GIC). You will also want to have a few hundred dollars (or more) in cash stored in a safe place in your home. This is to ensure you can still buy necessities if there is a natural disaster that knocks out the ability to pay for goods and services with debit and credit cards. Think of floods, hurricanes, earthquakes, terrorist attacks, and cyber crime. Canada is not immune.

To start your emergency fund, set up an automatic transfer to a high-interest savings account. A "make-it-automatic," "pay-yourself-first," or similar program, whatever you want to call it, is fine: just do it. Even if your automatic savings plan is only $25 a week to start, start it. Rome wasn't built in a day. Don't over-think it.

What if you don't have retirement savings and do have lots of debt? Credit card interest might cost you 28% per year, and a high-interest savings account might be earning you only 1%. Does it make sense to have $10,000 sitting in cash when you owe that much on a credit card? Of course not.

The recommended emergency fund of 3 months' worth of expenses really only applies if you don't have high-interest debt. But, if you *do* have high-interest debt, that doesn't mean you should have absolutely *no* emergency fund. It just needs to be smaller. Way smaller.

If you have maxed-out credit cards, you are on a path that could lead at any moment to financial disaster. One more unexpected expense and you could find yourself missing bill payments, or even heading to a dreaded payday-loan operation that provides an advance on your paycheque at interest rates that would make a credit card blush. Eventually, this path can lead to bankruptcy.

If you feel as though you're headed in this direction, you have to decide how much longer you want to keep going before you turn back. Sooner or later, you're likely to find you have no more credit available, and that's a hard place to be in. If you have reached this point already, you might have thought about what would happen if you lost your job, right at this most inopportune time. It would guarantee financial ruin in a matter of weeks.

At some point, you'll heed the wake-up call yourself. Enough is enough. Time to set off in a new direction and start climbing your way out of debt. With planning and luck, that decision will lead eventually to the day when you find yourself running a surplus (see Chapter 2), and then using those surplus funds to aggressively pay down debt (see Chapter 3). The hard truth is that, if you are carrying credit card debt, whatever credit you have left *is* your emergency fund. This is not ideal, but so long as you're paying down that debt, then you're moving in the right direction. Don't let up once you've freed up a few thousand dollars in credit—you need to get rid of it all.

People often wonder if there is a magic financial solution that will get them out of a certain predicament. In this case, there isn't. You have to do the financial sit-ups you know you have to do, and it's going to be painful for a while.

While 3 months' worth of expenses as an emergency fund is not feasible for people with high-interest debt, a smaller fund is still necessary. You should aim to have a few hundred dollars in cash stored in a safe spot in the home as just mentioned. But it has to remain untouched, except for extreme emergencies.

WILLS AND POWERS OF ATTORNEY

Most people already know what a will is. When you die, a will explains how you want your estate to be taken care of and distributed. If you have young children, you can use your will to assign a guardian to take care of them and ensure that there is money available to help the guardian in case you and your spouse die. (That money, incidentally, might come from a life insurance policy.)

A power of attorney (POA) is a document that gives someone else the ability to act on your behalf in case you become incapacitated and unable to make decisions for yourself. If, for some reason, you ended up in a coma, for example, a power of attorney would come into force. There are two main types of powers of attorney: power of attorney for finances (or property) and power of attorney for health care.

Power of Attorney for Finances (or Property)

If you get sick or have an accident and become incapacitated, you still have bills to pay. If you want to make sure your finances are being attended to, you need someone to act on your behalf—an "attorney." Note that in this context, an attorney is not a lawyer. It's just another person.

This attorney would be responsible for making financial decisions while you are unable to make them yourself. For example, if your mortgage comes up for renewal, it might just roll over at the offered rate for a new 5-year term, whereas you might have wanted to shop around for a new mortgage provider and a better rate (or other features). Perhaps you receive a tax refund from the Canada Revenue Agency: instead of just sitting in cash, your attorney could use the funds to help your child pay for school.

Power of Attorney for Health Care

A power of attorney for health care is similar in nature, except the decisions made by the attorney reflect your medical treatment in case you can't make those decisions on your own due to incapacitation.

A "living will" is a document that may eliminate the need for an attorney to act on your behalf. It's a document that outlines the kind of medical treatment you wish to receive in dire circumstances. For example, you might indicate that you have no desire to remain on life support if it's essentially all that is keeping you alive. This directive can also be included in the power of attorney for health care as a guide for the attorney.

These documents may have slightly different names and nuances in different provinces. For example, some provinces use the term "advance directive," others use "health care directive," and so on. These differences underscore the need for a lawyer to provide professional advice. The cost of having them drawn up differs a lot between law firms, for a variety of reasons. A simple will and set of powers of attorney can be about $400 on the low end. Documents that deal with more complex situations can run a few thousand dollars. I'm sure everyone has seen the do-it-yourself will kits advertised on TV or on the internet. For a sum as little as $30 you can create your own will. First of all, you need to know that some kits are better than others. Second, if you have anything that isn't plain vanilla with respect to your living situation or estate, you might not create a will that either does what you intended or holds up in court if someone contests it.

If you die without a will, the courts will appoint someone to administer your estate. This may or may not be done according to what you would have preferred. But if you're single, with no dependants, and have a simple estate, it's probably not the end of the world. But once you have a major life event, such as getting married, getting a will drafted and signed moves up the list of your priorities really fast.

And if you have kids, run, don't walk, to get it set up. I have met countless couples in the last few years who have told me how they waited years after the birth of their first child to get their wills set up. I don't need to finger-wag here. If you're in that situation, you already know what you have to do.

Powers of attorney and/or your living will are a different story. If you become incapacitated and don't have a spouse or children, you still need to have your finances managed in case your incapacitation is prolonged. You may still have healthcare directives you want followed. Getting your powers of attorney set up can cost just over $100 if you get them done on their own.

These documents don't do you any good if no one knows about them. It's important to let your loved ones know where you keep them. When you get everything set up, call your parents, siblings, guardians for your children, whomever, and let them know where to find these documents. They should ideally be kept with all your important financial and medical papers. Note: think twice about using a safety deposit box for some important documents. A bank will be very reluctant to release the contents of these boxes to anyone other than the owner. That's a hassle you can avoid by using an alternate, safe storage location.

A PAUSE FOR THOUGHT

Let's take a moment before continuing. We've just gone over Rule 1. Along the way, I've given you some not-so-subtle hints to get the ball rolling on how to disaster-proof your life. Did you call an insurance agent? What about a lawyer? If you haven't, remember that you have no control over what life throws at you or when it gets thrown. Don't make the mistake of thinking that bad things can't happen to you. And don't delay.

Perhaps you are waiting to finish reading the book before you start putting any plans into action. And maybe that's because you worry that you don't have the money to pay for a will, powers of attorney, insurance policies, and an emergency fund. Booking a meeting with a lawyer or an insurance agent doesn't mean you have to fork over money today. It might be a month or longer between now and when you have to shoulder that cost. You just need to meet with someone and get the process started. You should be able to finish this book before you have to make any commitments or sign any documents. If you are serious about your money, that's enough time to figure out how to pay for these costs.

There are only five rules. You have to follow them all if you want that easy A.

Still not convinced? Contact me on Twitter (@preetbanerjee) and let me know what's got you stuck.

CHAPTER TWO

RULE 2: SPEND LESS THAN YOU EARN

Spending less than you earn is the cornerstone of financial stability. It makes possible the elimination of money stress and is the beginning of wealth creation. Once you've disaster-proofed your life to guard against emergencies that could happen tomorrow to completely derail your financial life, the next thing you have to focus on is running a surplus: having some money left over at the end of the month instead of some month left over at the end of the money. I can't emphasize enough the importance of this simple rule.

If you want to create wealth, the fundamental formula is as follows:

$$\text{Surplus} \times \text{Time} = \text{Wealth}$$

Where is that whimpering party favour that sounds like a dying duck? This formula is about as unsexy a concept as you'll find in any personal finance book. People want to know how to pick stocks, what ETFs to buy, how to keep costs low, and so on. Should they invest in a TFSA? Or an RRSP? Or both? And if both, then what percentage goes into what? Those are all great questions to ask, but only after you realize the importance of this simple formula, and how it is ultimately much more important than the answers to all those other questions put together.

If you don't run a surplus, you won't ever have to worry about what to put in your investment portfolio because there won't be one. Who cares about the difference in taxation of dividends and capital gains in your portfolio? *What portfolio?* If you want to become more fit, you have to work out and eat healthy foods. In order to become an investor, first you must become a saver. Both propositions are equally boring and equally true. There's another parallel between physical and financial fitness. That is that while the concepts are simple, they can be incredibly hard to implement. We know what we have to do. It's not rocket science. All it takes is willpower.

I'll talk about the motivational aspect of running a surplus in Chapter 5. For now, I'll show you some practical ways to actually run a surplus. First, you need to learn how to budget—either with a spreadsheet or, for those who find spreadsheets scary, without one.

HOW TO BUDGET WITH A SPREADSHEET

There is no shortage of spreadsheet templates on the internet. They are all pretty much equal, but some are more equal than others. I'll save you some time. The next two pages show an example of budgeting spreadsheets. If you would like this in electronic format, just go to Squawkfox.com (written by Kerry K. Taylor) and in the top right-hand side of the page there will be a "search" box. Type in "how to make a budget." The search engine will take you to a listing of pages on Kerry's site. Any of the first few non-advertisement links will take you to her ridiculously awesome section titled "Financial Planning Series: How to Make a Budget." It will walk you through the process of creating a proper budget, but here's what you have to do:

1. Figure out your old budget.
2. Figure out a new budget.
3. Start tracking your spending more diligently.
4. Save the savings.
5. Plan for non-monthly expenses.

1. Figure Out Your Old Budget

The budget itself is simply what comes in the door (income) compared to what goes out the door (expenses) over a set period of time (usually a month). Your old budget is easy to figure out. You probably have a good

Figure 2.1: The Squawkfox spreadsheet makes starting a budget easy.

	Jan	Feb	Mar	Apr	May	Jun	Jul	Aug	Sep	Oct	Nov	Dec	Total	Monthly Avg.
Income:														
Salary														
Bonus														
Investments														
Other														
Total														
Home Expenses:														
Rent/Mortgage														
Home Insurance														
Maintenance														
Property Taxes														
Other														
Total														
Transportation:														
Car Payments														
Licence & Registration														
Car Insurance														
Fuel														
Maintenance														
Bus/Transit Pass														
Other														
Total														
Utilities:														
Electricity														
Gas/Heating Oil														
Telephone														
Cellphones														
Internet														
Television														
Water														
Other														
Total														
Medical:														
Health Insurance														
Dental														
Prescriptions														
Glasses & Contacts														
Life Insurance														
Other														
Total														

Financial:
Bank Fees
Interest Payments
Debt Repayment
Credit Card Repayment
Emergency Fund Savings
Retirement Savings
Income Taxes Due
Other
Total

Enjoyment:
Gifts
Entertainment
Vacations
Pets
Hobbies
Restaurants
Holiday Expenses
Other
Total

Routine Expenses:
Groceries
Clothing
Other
Total

Family:
Childcare
School Supplies
Tuition
Books
Activities
Allowance
Other
Total

Total Income
Total Expenses
Difference

Source: Kerry K. Taylor, Squawkfox.com

idea what your income is, especially if you get a regular paycheque, as most people do. And figuring out your expenses is pretty easy these days. Just gather up your credit card and debit card statements and plug in all the transactions for each month for as far back as you like. I recommend aiming for at least 3 months. Create as many categories as you like, or use Kerry's spreadsheet. Now add up all the expenses. If the expenses are more than your income, you are running a deficit. If they are the same, your budget is balanced. And if they are less than your income, you are running a surplus. If you make a lot of cash transactions, you can mark those transactions as "cash" for the time being. Mark any automated teller machine (ATM) withdrawal in the cash category, unless you have a receipt that tells you exactly where it was spent.

I want to urge caution here. Some people will find it frustrating to go back in time to add up expenses because they may know they are missing items. Not to worry: you can afford to be a bit sloppy here. It's about the process at this point rather than the exact numbers. Budgeting is an ongoing endeavour and you'll get better at it. Especially once you start diligently tracking expenses going forward.

So now you've figured out your old budget. It can be a sobering experience.

Even as you fill in all the items you have purchased in the various categories, you will probably be disgusted to see just how much money gets spent on what you might have thought were minor luxuries. Think: coffee, lunches with people at work, dinners out and meals ordered in, movies, etc. When you're not tracking these things, a few dollars here and a few dollars there seem harmless. But the daily consumer of a latte or cappuccino can be spending $80 per month if he or she grabs one on the way to work every day. Some days you skip breakfast and grab a snack with your morning drink. If you do, then that sum might average closer to $100 per month. Someone who eats at a food court near their office every day might easily spend a few hundred dollars per month. The little indulgences add up in a hurry.

Don't forget all your debt payments. Are you paying $500 a month in credit card bills, but your balance isn't going down? (Or worse, is it going up every month?) Do you have an interest-only payment on a line of credit? Student loans? When you add up all your debts (mortgage, credit cards, loans, etc.), if that number isn't getting smaller every month, you are not running a surplus (assuming you are not stockpiling cash at the same time as your debts are increasing).

Especially if it's the first time they've ever done

it, most people are flabbergasted by what they see in at least one category, if not more. I promise you will instantly cut back your spending simply as a result of tracking it for the first time and becoming more aware of what's happening.

2. Figure Out a New Budget

The real magic comes when you decide to create a new budget. As you look at each category, you have to pause and ask yourself how you can reduce that number.

There are some payments you can't modify easily, such as a mortgage or rent payment, but there are many others you have immediate control over. Maybe you have a bundled TV, internet, and phone package. Call up your provider and ask how you can save money. You would be surprised how often this results in savings without much effort. A new package may give you all the features you want at a lower cost.

If you are spending $500 on restaurants, figure out what your new budget should be and how you plan to achieve it. Do you go out less often? Eat at less expensive restaurants? The same thinking can be applied in every category. How much are you paying in bank fees? How much do you spend on groceries? Everything. Your new budget should be a guide for what you allow yourself to spend in these various categories every month.

3. Start Tracking Your Spending More Diligently

As mentioned earlier, you may find that going back in time to figure out your spending is tedious and perhaps imprecise. But it will be much easier going forward if you keep these tips in mind:

a. Get a box, bowl, folder, jar, or whatever, and put it near your front door in a spot you always walk past. This is where you are going to dump all your receipts and bills every day.

b. From now on, don't hand someone cash, a debit card, or a credit card without getting a receipt back. Collect your receipts. Even if you are buying a pack of gum for 98 cents, get a receipt for it. Put it in your receipt jar.

c. Anytime a bill comes in the mail, even if it is a notice to let you know a payment was made automatically, put it with all your receipts for the month.

d. At the end of the month, enter all your expenses in your spreadsheet. Was there a big change from the previous month? Also, remember that if you have a cash withdrawal for $20, and receipts showing where that $20 was spent, don't enter the expense twice.

It should go without saying that if you were spending $500 per month on restaurants, and you set a new budget of $300 per month, and then managed to spend just $200 per month, that's fantastic! There are some cases where the goal of saving money becomes exciting. (Yes, I wrote that with a straight face. You'll see.)

You'll note that my simple approach to budgeting is to figure out your old budget, create a new budget, start tracking expenses more diligently, and then to save the savings. "Save the savings" means exactly what it says.

4. Save the Savings

I have often heard of people who save money by cutting back on one unnecessary expense only to use the savings for something else that is just as frivolous. For example, they might reduce that spending on clothing from $100 to $50 a month. But all of a sudden, $50 a month is now being spent on upgrading their cable package.

Consider someone who starts a new fitness regimen. Maybe they are lifting weights or running for 30 minutes three times a week. But if they feel famished after their workout and head off to grab some fast food, also three times a week, they might not notice any change in their physical appearance. Had they not been working out, perhaps those treats would have added a chin. On the flip side, adding the workout while skipping the additional junk food might have resulted in a positive change to their physique.

It's the same with money.

Maybe you have negotiated the interest rate on your next mortgage to be 0.5 percentage points below the renewal rate you were initially offered. But unless you have a concrete plan for those savings, they may get spent without you even noticing. In order for your sacrifices and hard-fought-for deals to mean something to your bottom line, you need to put the savings to productive use. Paying down debt, investing, and purchasing insurance you have been procrastinating about are all good examples.

Everyone has seen those opportunity-cost calculations that show you how reducing your expenses on activity X could turn into $100,000 in 25 years if you put the money in an investment portfolio. Generally speaking, the rate-of-return assumptions are on the high side to motivate you. That's all fine and dandy, but again, it assumes you save the savings.

As a teenager, I remember seeing a commercial that showed a smoker blowing up a Porsche 911 Cabriolet as a high-impact visualization of the opportunity cost of smoking. According to the Smoking and Health Action Foundation, the average carton of cigarettes currently costs between $70.18 and $106.09, depending on the province or territory you live in. If we average those extremes, and take into account that a carton contains 200 cigarettes, we can calculate the cost of a cigarette at about 45 cents. I'll make some simple assumptions for my own high-impact analysis: a smoker starts smoking a pack a day at 15, paying $9.00 for a pack. If, instead of smoking, he or she directed that money to a moderately aggressive investment portfolio, the long-term, after-inflation rate of return would have been 3%. That works out to more than $375,000 of opportunity cost in today's dollars by the time he or she reaches 65. That kind of money buys a nice car. But this kind of financial return is possible only *if you save the savings.*

If you are making a sacrifice to truly improve your finances, you must set up automatic transfers from your chequing account to your savings account that mimics your old spending pattern. For example, if you are giving up a pack of cigarettes a day, you can set up a daily $9 transfer. If you are skipping ordering wine when eating out on Friday nights, you could set up a weekly $25 transfer. (Make sure that your banking package covers all the extra transactions before setting these up.)

Not everyone is ready to go cold turkey by giving up their pricey habits, but unless you actually save the savings, you're not making progress. It's like eating a bacon double cheeseburger after a 10K run: that's a lot of pain with no real gain.

5. Plan for Non-Monthly Expenses

Your surplus should go mainly to paying down high-interest debt aggressively (see Chapter 3). But part of it can be used to build up a short-term savings fund for the non-monthly expenses we always encounter, such as holidays and birthday gifts. If you forecast these expenditures on your calendar, you can set aside cash to pay for them when the time comes. For example, if you've forecasted that you will spend an average of $1,000 per year for various holidays, birthday and anniversary presents, then one twelfth of $1,000 needs to be put away each month into your short-term savings fund.

Note that until your high-interest debt is zero, you need to cool it on what you think you can spend on presents and anything frivolous. Cutting back on gift-giving is difficult to do when it comes to the children in your life, but if you and your spouse have high-interest debt, the best present you can give each other is paying down debt. It's a tough sell if you're not both on board, so talk it over, and make sure to say it was all my idea.

HOW TO BUDGET WITHOUT A SPREADSHEET

There's no shortage of how-to-budget resources in the world. And everybody knows they're not supposed to spend more than they earn. So one could assume that a low savings rate is not due to an inability to add and subtract, given that most Canadians have the Grade 3 skill set required. So what exactly is the problem?

For a lot of people, meticulously formulating and tracking a household budget works about as well as me on a dance floor. Believe me, it ain't pretty! But I'm a veritable Fred Astaire with a spreadsheet.

There was a time when I would indeed grab a receipt for every single thing I purchased and enter it into my spreadsheet. It was great for finding out where I was spending more than I thought, and it allowed me to save some money by consciously cutting back where appropriate. Cutting back meant that I had cash left over at the end of the month. Which was great. But for those of you who are bad on the budgeting dance floor, take solace. Here's why I abandoned spreadsheets and never looked back: human beings have an uncanny ability to adapt.

If you receive notice of a rent increase from your landlord or your mortgage payment goes up on your next term, you're not likely to move. You're more likely to stay where you are and suck up the increase. Ditto for gas. The price of gasoline has skyrocketed, and yet we still have traffic jams. People adapt. Remember when gas first hit $1 per litre on the way up? People went crazy. If it hit $1 per litre today, we'd be dancing in the streets. But if gas did in fact fall to $1 per litre, not many of us would suddenly start saving the savings. We would simply spend the extra money elsewhere.

So, for many people, the trick to saving may be to force yourself to adapt. Instead of waiting to see if there is a surplus at the end of the month, have your desired savings taken out of your bank account automatically on the day after you get paid, and focus on not getting into the red before the next payday. You will adapt.

Let me reiterate this simple two-step plan for budgeting without a spreadsheet:

1. Save at the beginning of the month.
2. Don't let your bank account sink below zero by the end of the month.

Avoid using your credit card if you have an unpaid balance. Remember, you have to cut back until all your high-interest debt is gone. Sometimes we think we need something when in fact it is simply a want. Be vigilant! If there is no alternative except to use your credit card when you're out shopping, you had better be able to transfer an equivalent amount from your chequing account to your credit card when you get home. If you can't stick to this short-cut plan, then sorry: you're gonna have to suck it up and use the spreadsheet after all.

To make the no-spreadsheet system work, you need to save an amount at the beginning of the month that feels like it would be a bit of a stretch. You can't get lazy about it. Well, not any more lazy than not having to use a spreadsheet. If you are worried because you're already stretching your income, the worst-case scenario is that, after a few months, you have money in your savings account and an offsetting amount of money owing on credit cards. You can take the cash from the savings and pay down the money owing. But I would be willing to bet that most people who think they are stretched already will suddenly find they have savings without extra money owing simply because they adapted to the new normal.

Some people do fine with spreadsheets and that's great. But for others, simple budgeting problems seem insurmountable because they over-think them. Stop thinking, and just do. Some call it "pay yourself first," others say "make it automatic." I say, "Dance, cowboy!"

How much should you save? Here are a few pointers:

1. The traditional recommended savings figure is 10% of gross income, but that is for long-term savings. If you save only 10% of income and end up spending the accumulated savings once a year, you will have done nothing to prepare for retirement.

2. Given that 10% should be the minimum to invest for the future, you need to determine the percentage you'll need to tuck away as short-term savings for the year.

3. Short-term savings covers lump-sum expenses such as vacations, birthday and holiday presents, and other non-monthly items. If you can earn interest on saving up for these expenses ahead of time, instead of paying interest to finance them after the fact, you'll be one step ahead of the game.

4. Increase your automatic savings every January first. Remember to increase it just a little bit more than you think you can handle. You can always pare back if it's too tough. But be honest about whether it is too tough, or you aren't tough enough.

5. Be sure to increase your savings when your income goes up.

BANK ACCOUNTS FOR COUPLES

One of the questions I am asked most often is how to arrange bank accounts for a couple. Should they be separate? Should you just have one joint account?

Rarely is there a one-size-fits-all answer for any question about money, so I'll preface this by saying that if you have a system that works well for you, more power to you. One big joint account might be fine ... for you. Completely separate bank accounts might also be fine ... for you.

But, if you have never really thought about it before, then here is what I suggest for people who have made a long-term commitment to each other and don't feel confident that they have a handle on things: three bank accounts. One joint account for your regular household inflows and outflows, and two separate personal accounts for your "mad money."

The Joint Account

Setting up one joint account into which both your paycheques are deposited is Step One. All your regular expenses, such as the mortgage payment, utilities, phone bills, insurance premiums, car payments, and so on, are paid from this account. That's Step Two. Step Three is to make sure that at the end of each month there is a surplus. If not, you have to fix that before you do anything else. Your monthly long-term investment or savings contributions should come from this one joint account as well.

Separate Personal Accounts

The personal accounts are for your indulgences. The point of these accounts is that you don't have to be accountable to your spouse or partner for what you spend this money on—so long as you don't go over your "allowance." As a couple, you should determine how much money gets transferred to these accounts in the first place.

Perhaps you've decided that each person gets $300 transferred monthly to the personal account. One person uses that $300 by buying fancy coffees and going out for lunch at work. The other person might not use it up at all, and their account builds up slowly over time. The person with the savings should feel fine about using them to buy big-ticket items every once in a while, such as electronic gadgets, jewellery, etc.

This three-account system is a good starter system, especially if you haven't been talking about your personal finances with your significant other before. You'll both have a better handle on the household finances as you establish the overall budget in the joint account, but you'll also make those guilty pleasures feel a lot less guilty.

CRASH TESTING YOUR FINANCES TO START SAVING MONEY

Christmas happens every year. And every year people pile up debt on their credit cards.

One area of household budgeting that tends to catch people out are the non-regular expenses. People are less likely to spend $100 per month on clothing than they are to spend $600 twice a year. It's the same for holiday expenses. We don't spend $10 per month on toys. We buy toys worth $120 in December.

The problem is that many people are making ends meet only for their monthly expenses, so these non-monthly expenses can catch them out. We have the gifts to shop for before the holidays and the sales to tempt us after they're over. Alcohol consumption rises in December with all the family get-togethers (perhaps to *survive* the family get-togethers) and then, as we enter January, we are tempted by the prospect of tanning on a beach at an all-inclusive resort.

Taken together, you could have two or three consecutive months in which you find yourself spending upwards of $1,000 per month more than usual.

The norm is to spend the money and then pay it off after the fact. We suffer from debt remorse for a while, which usually means the debt gets paid off, but every time that happens, a new cause for celebration appears just around the corner. Think, for example, of

Valentine's Day and the reverse sale on flowers that goes with it (it's the one time all year when you can be sure the price of petals goes up). The temptation to make exceptional expenditures never ends. But we keep treading water.

If we can save up ahead of time, instead of financing a purchase after the fact, then we can earn interest instead of paying it. Our overall cost comes down, not to mention our stress level. But, of course, flipping that switch is easier said than done. Mostly it means you have to delay gratification for something, at least for a little while.

If you find you're not really motivated to put off spending, think about this: some experts believe a worldwide recession is in the cards. Pretend you lost your job today and you won't find work again until the end of the year. Your immediate response would be to tighten the purse strings, take any leftover money, and put it into a savings account. You might switch from name to no-name brands and buy cheaper items at the grocery store. There would be no going out to fancy dinners or movies. No buying songs on iTunes and no lattes. If there's no penalty incurred for putting the movie channels on hold, you could try that too. Only spend on needs, not wants. Try this and see how far you can take it.

Think of it as a kind of fire drill. No one knows if

and when they might lose their job. It could happen for a variety of reasons beyond your control. Perhaps the prospect of such an occurrence is enough to motivate you to flip the switch from spender to saver though a temporary crash test. If you try it, and if you are successful, the key is to continue to be one step ahead by constantly saving up for the next event instead of always paying off the last one.

It would be tough to actually simulate a total loss of income, but try to cut as much spending as you can on a temporary basis. There are some expenses that simply can't be cut on a short-term basis. Write them down so that you have an idea what your actual minimum expenses would be if you had a significant loss of income. Here are some other tips:

- Pinch your pennies hard for 3 months on luxuries and actually cut out some fat. That money goes into a savings account.
- Calculate what you would change in theory if you really did lose your job. Could you downgrade your car? House?
- What penalties would you face for cancelling long-term contracts (think: cellphones, gym memberships, everything).
- After you've figured out your minimum living expenses, calculate how long you could survive.

This exercise might provide the motivation you're looking for to switch from financing to saving. We can hope it will only ever be a drill.

TO SAVE OR NOT TO SAVE?

To save or not to save? That used to be the question. But given that the economy has been weak ever since the credit crisis, some observers are debating a different question: to spend or not to spend? Because more spending is better for the economy.

The problem is that the average Canadian household has been gradually spending more and saving less. The Vanier Institute of the Family's research reveals that the ratio of debt to income has been steadily increasing for the past 20 years, from 93% to 150%. The savings-to-income ratio shows the opposite trend, decreasing from 13% to 4.2%.

Some might suggest people are spending more solely because the necessities of life have increased in cost. And while it's true that housing costs more, food and gas are on the rise, and incomes don't seem to be rising as quickly as they once were, that's only part of the story. Lower interest rates have made it cheaper to borrow and less rewarding to save. And that's only given some people more rope with which to ultimately hang themselves if something goes wrong. They might lose their jobs. Or maybe debt payments will increase with interest-rate hikes leaving them with even less money to spend.

But not all spending is bad spending. We need people to spend to generate sales for business. If these companies don't have sales, they could lay off workers, which means even lower sales, which could lead to more layoffs, and so on.

Ironically, some people argue that too much saving is bad. The paradox of thrift is that a higher average saving rate leads to lower overall savings. This is because higher saving means lower spending, which means a curtailment in job growth. Those potential new workers—the ones not hired—could be saving part of their income too, but since they don't exist, their savings don't exist either.

So do you spend to do your bit for the economy? Or do you rein it in to save yourself?

If present trends continue, eventually we'll get to a point where we can't spend anymore at all. A rising debt-to-income ratio means we are spending future income today. That can only go on so long before there's a rude awakening. Just ask the U.S. government about their recent fiscal-cliff and sequester fiascos. So perhaps the question should be rephrased: to save yourself or not to save yourself? Then I think the answer becomes apparent. The best thing you can do is to save yourself. If you run out of the ability to spend one day, that is worse for the economy than being able to spend a little for a long, long time.

Are interest rates too low to make saving worthwhile? Low interest rates have led many people to wonder if they should bother saving their money. While anemic returns on short-term guaranteed income certificates (GICs) and savings accounts provide little growth, present conditions aren't actually as different from what some regard as the heyday of higher savings rates.

As I write, the going rate on a one-year GIC from a big bank is about 1%. Assuming the investor is in a 35% tax bracket, an initial investment of $1,000 would grow to $1,010 by the end of the year, lose $3.50 to tax, and an additional $26.17 to inflation (currently running at 2.6%). So this low-interest rate environment leads to a decrease in purchasing power of 1.97% overall, and the original $1,000 can now buy only $980.33 worth of goods.

Back in 1980 interest rates were higher, but so was inflation. You could've picked up a one-year GIC paying perhaps 13%, while inflation was running at about 10%. Assuming the same marginal tax rate of 35%, an initial investment of $1,000 grew to $1,130 before losing $45.50 to tax. The remaining $1,084.50 then lost $108.45 to inflation to leave you with a decrease in purchasing power of 2.4%. Your original $1,000 could buy only $976.05 worth of goods at the end of 1980.

Saving inside a registered plan, such as an RRSP or TFSA, negates the tax drag, and, because these tax-sheltered accounts are more prevalent now than they were in the early 1980s, one could argue that saving money now makes more sense than it did back then. You can disregard the math though. People whom I would consider to be financially successful grasp a few simpler money-management concepts. One of those concepts is simply to be a habitual saver.

I know many individuals who are well versed in financial theory, read all the books, and who could quite frankly run rings around the average financial advisor with respect to their knowledge of the nitty-gritty details of investing, but that doesn't necessarily translate into financial success. To be an investor, first you must be a saver.

Once saving has become a habit, if you are still unhappy with the growth of your money, the low returns on safe investments can be exchanged for potentially higher returns with riskier investments, if you so desire. But until you are a saver, there's no point in counting those chickens: the eggs have not yet hatched. You don't have to worry about putting all your eggs in one basket when there are no eggs to begin with.

Speaking of developing good habits, it never hurts to start young. Rob Carrick, a personal finance columnist with *The Globe and Mail*, wrote a great book, *How Not to Move Back in with Your Parents: The Young Person's Guide to Financial Empowerment*. This is on my recommended list and is actually appropriate for parents too, because it can help them to help their children navigate their personal finances.

If you would like to learn about a whole bunch of specific ways you can cut your expenses, pick up *397 Ways to Save Money* by Kerry K. Taylor (yes, the same person behind Squawkfox.com). She is one of the most widely read personal finance bloggers in the world. Read her blog and buy her book. You can thank me later.

CHAPTER THREE

RULE 3: AGGRESSIVELY PAY DOWN HIGH-INTEREST DEBT

Thou shalt not carry credit card balances!

Debt can cripple people's finances. It can ruin marriages and relationships. It can make you miserable. And it can handcuff you, keeping you from realizing your financial potential. This applies to any high-interest debt. It could be a charge card, department store card, whatever.

When you have a lot of debt, the amount of cash flow it ties up on a monthly basis is painful to calculate. Especially when it's in the form of high-interest debt. There are families spending thousands of dollars a month in interest payments on credit cards. I recently met a family with more than $50,000 in credit card debt. At an average 28% rate of interest, they are paying $14,000 per year, or $1,166.67 per month, just to carry the debt. They might pay this forever if they don't pay it down. After 10 years, they will have paid $140,000 in interest without putting a dent in the debt itself.

They didn't start out with $50,000 in credit card debt, it crept up on them over time. And there are many people in the same situation.

Even paying $200 per month in interest on a credit card, charge card, department-store card, or whatever-card debt is deflating. Most people at some point wonder to themselves, "What could I do with the money I'm losing to interest every month?" If you can't pay off your credit card balance in full every month, you are using debt irresponsibly.

Credit cards have some fine rewards programs, but they work out to an equivalent of roughly 2% of what you spend. Carry a balance and you could be paying 28% interest in perpetuity. In that case, those incentives to use your credit card to earn travel rewards are *costing* you money, not *making* you money. So forget about rewards programs as a reason to use credit cards if you carry a balance.

I often come across people with multiple maxed-out, or nearly maxed-out, credit cards. They might have a secured line of credit, car loan, student loan, mortgage, and almost invariably a loan to a furniture store. They are drowning in debt. In some cases, they don't stop spending more than they earn until they run out of credit.

They all had the ability to stop overspending on their own. The fact that their overspending stopped because they were denied access to more credit means someone else is in control, not them.

The cost of carrying debt in perpetuity is astounding. A family that carries an average $5,000 balance during their working career will spend about $70,000 in credit card interest. Seventy thousand dollars is a lot of money to pay for spending $5,000 once. This kind of overspending is not unusual. According to the U.S. Federal Reserve, in late 2012 the average credit card balance for American households that had a balance owing was just over $15,000. Eventually, people can get to a point where they've had enough. They decide they want to be the ones in control and are ready to do what it takes to run a surplus and pay down their debts. But sometimes they are confused about how to tackle it all.

Assuming you are now running a surplus, where do you direct your funds to give you the best bang for your buck?

1. TRANSFER HIGH-INTEREST BALANCES TO LOW-INTEREST BALANCES

If you have room on a line of credit, start by transferring the credit card balances there. A credit card with a

$5,000 balance at 28% interest is costing you more than $115 in interest per month. Transfer that to a line of credit that charges 5%, and you've saved yourself almost $100 per month—which *must* go towards paying down the line of credit. The next thing you need to do is call your credit card company and have the credit limit reduced or have the card cancelled to prevent you from getting into trouble again. I know some people may rely on credit as their emergency reserve, but I also know they have multiple credit cards.

Once you've shifted your balances to the lowest-interest-rate facilities, you need to ensure that you don't use your credit cards, or get a new loan, or borrow in any other way, until you're rehabilitated. Freeze your cards in a block of ice, cut them up, do whatever it takes to prevent you from using them.

2. DEVELOP A PLAN OF ATTACK FOR PAYING DOWN YOUR DEBT

Create a list of all your debts, not including the mortgage. If you have three credit cards, all with a balance, list them. Many people have no rhyme or reason in their approach to paying their credit card bills. If they have $600 per month dedicated to paying off the three cards, they may pay $200 to each. That's not ideal. You need to focus on paying them off one at a time, while still meeting your minimum payments on each one (and slightly more than just the minimum is okay). That might mean payments of $50 per month to two of the cards and $500 per month to one card. The question is, which card do you pay off first?

You can either pay off the cards in order of highest interest rate first and lowest interest rate last, or begin with the card that has the lowest balance and deal with the one that has the highest balance last. Once one card is paid off, you focus on the next card until they are all paid off.

If you pay off the card with the highest interest rate, you're reducing your overall interest payments fastest and, from a pure numbers standpoint, it's the best way to go. It makes you debt-free the fastest, although usually not by a landslide. But, in my experience, people respond better to paying off the card with the smallest balance first. The psychological victory they enjoy by slaying a credit card once and for all is a powerful motivator.

Now, the next card in line receives a $550 monthly payment ($500 plus the $50 minimum payment you were making before). Once that's paid off, the last card gets $600 per month. This is commonly referred to as the "debt snowball" method. Unless you have strong objections to the approach, use the snowball method and pick the debt that will get paid off the fastest, regardless of interest rate. Don't over-think it, just do it.

A word of caution to anyone thinking about taking credit card and other debt balances and adding them onto your mortgage. The idea that you can "consolidate" debt into your mortgage is sometimes offered as an attractive solution to a heavy debt burden. The illustrations and calculations can show monthly increases of freed-up cash to the tune of hundreds of dollars, because a 25-year loan at 4% for $10,000 in debt doesn't cost as much as an open-ended $10,000 balance on a credit card at 28%. Many see it as a fresh start. Just one debt payment—the mortgage, and no credit card debt.

But not everyone who consolidates their debts has learned their lesson. In many cases, they've just given themselves more rope with which to hang themselves. I've seen cases where people consolidated multiple times because they kept on overspending. They may have started with a $250,000 mortgage, and 10 years later it's $300,000: they can do this only owing to the fact that real estate has been increasing in value steadily for the better part of two decades. That increase allows them to use the built-up equity in their home to finance dumb spending decisions. They clean up their credit card debt only to rack it up again. Wash, rinse, repeat. That's great advice for shampooing your hair, awful advice for managing your debt.

Don't say you haven't been warned. A debt Armageddon is entirely possible in Canada's future.

IT'S NOT THAT SIMPLE

As with all of the fundamentals of managing your personal finances, the theory and formulas are far from being rocket science. Unfortunately, it's not the theory that trips us up: it's the implementation. You have to understand that your life is going to have to change if you want to see actual change. Prescriptions for getting your finances in order are just like the thousands of diets and workout regimens out there: the information is useless until you exert discipline and self-control in order to follow the steps.

A numbers-based solution to a psychologically rooted problem won't resonate with some people. You either have to fall far enough for the problem to stress and consume you, or you have to educate yourself about just why you should hate debt with a passion.* It's kind

---

* I had the honour of being invited to give a TEDx Talk recently. For those of you who are not familiar with TED Talks, they are the product of a non-profit organization that challenges speakers to "give the talk of their life" in 18 minutes or less. It's about spreading ideas and challenging what we think. A TEDx event is a locally organized TED event and my alma mater, the University of Toronto Scarborough (UTSC), hosted one. My presentation was about why we should start hating debt again—because

of ironic when you think about it: *some people take on debt in order to consume things until debt consumes them.*

If you want to spend more, save more. If you understand and embrace this fundamental precept—that you should be earning interest instead of paying it—you'll be better off than most people. I'll end this chapter with a few thoughts about debt.

Financing a $35,000-car might cost you $43,000 after factoring in the interest you pay, but saving up for it in advance might earn you $1,000 in interest, so you only have to put aside $34,000. That's a $9,000 difference out of your pocket for that same car. The average person might own nine cars in a lifetime. So the average couple might own 18 cars: 18 × $9,000 = $162,000. That's four more cars you could have bought. Or fancier cars. Or you might find that when you have $35,000 sitting in your short-term savings account, you're less likely to buy a $35,000 car, because it's harder to part with $35,000 of cash than it is to buy a $35,000 car on credit. Then you have more money for other stuff.

---

people used to detest it in "the olden days." My talk is titled, "Why 2.5 Billion Heartbeats Might Change the Way You Think About Money," and I'll shamelessly suggest you watch it. Many people who were blasé about debt before the talk changed their minds about it, even though debt wasn't consuming them. You can search for the title online, or tweet me @preetbanerjee, and I'll send you the link.

Something to consider when you borrow money from a bank is that you aren't ultimately borrowing money from the bank. You're borrowing it from your future self. The bank is just the middleman between the two of you, and it charges you interest for its services. That interest charge means that not only are you spending your future income today, you get to spend less of it because there is a cost (interest) in order to access it. *Think of borrowing money as negotiating a pay-cut with your future self.* Eventually you will become your future self, and you might not be very happy.

So how does one go from financing cars to saving up for them in advance? Wouldn't that mean waiting for the loan on your current car to end and then saving up for the next car first? Yes, it would. In the first place, a car should last 10 years these days without breaking a sweat. And second, quite frankly, if it seems like a struggle to save up that money, that's a clear sign you can't afford a $35,000 car yet.

A car *has* to be reliable and get you from A to B. All entry-level compact cars fit that description. Anything above that is a luxury, a want. I don't care if you buy a top-of-the-line Mercedes-Benz—if you can afford it. But until you have mastered money, aim for the cheapest car that meets your regular needs. A friend of mine recently told me that he bought a slightly used sub-compact car for $12,000 because I gave him this rant a year ago. He earns well into six figures, but he said that, just by holding back on that car, all his money stress is gone. His friends couldn't care less that he isn't driving a luxury cruiser.

Everything that makes a cool car a cool car is not so cool after a few months of driving. Then it just gets you from A to B like every other car you've owned or will own. It's 90% in your head.

Gail Vaz-Oxlade's *Money Rules* is a great book with lots of common sense (and tough-love) approaches to managing your money (and your debts). This is another book I recommend for those who want to graduate up from an easy A to an A+, or who need help mastering some of the fundamentals.

CHAPTER FOUR

RULE 4: READ THE FINE PRINT

It amazes me to no end that people sign contracts without reading them. *From today onwards, you need to read every word on any document you put your signature on. Gym memberships, cellphone contracts, loan documents, you name it.* The fine print can be hard to read, but generally speaking, the smaller it is, the more likely it is to contain something that might give you second thoughts about signing.

Actually, what amazes me more is how many salespeople don't know what's in the contracts they ask you to sign. There have been a number of instances where I read the fine print on a contract, much to the chagrin of a salesperson, only to find out that they've either lied to me, were incompetent, or not up-to-date on the latest contracts.

When push comes to shove, the only leg you have to stand on in a dispute is what you put your name to. If you signed a contract, you are bound by it. A young couple told me recently about a vehicle they purchased a few years ago. They were excited that the last payment was due in a few months; they had been dying to make this final payment. They bought the vehicle at a time when they had a poor credit rating, so the interest rate on the loan was 12%. While they had it firmly in their minds that they would soon have no more payments to make, it turned out there was a balloon payment due on this last month (a final lump-sum payment) of more than $11,000. The couple was devastated. They had to finance the last debt payment because they didn't have the money.

Instead of first thoroughly reading the document when it was presented to them, they just signed it. Perhaps they were overly focused on the monthly payments, and perhaps the salesperson skimmed over the details. Either condition is irrelevant. Their signature bound them to the terms of that contract.

If you are worried about wasting someone's time while you read a contract in front of them, don't be. If there's a lot to read, chances are it's in your best interest to take the time to read it thoroughly. Ask to take the contract home to read on your own time (the delay might even cause you to second-guess your purchase). If you don't understand what it says, you can ask the salesperson, but it would be preferable to ask a friend, and if it's warranted, a lawyer.

Here's a real-world example of what reading the fine print can reveal: when I first started in the financial services, a friend of my branch manager died over the holiday season. The friend had both a private life insurance policy and a mortgage life insurance policy. A mortgage life insurance policy is one that might be offered to you by your bank (or other lender) when you are applying for a mortgage. You simply tick a box, the premium gets added to your mortgage payment, and if you die, you might reasonably expect to have the mortgage paid off. I'll dig into this type of insurance in more detail in Chapter 8, but for now, I'll just cut to the chase. The mortgage life insurance was underwritten at time of claim (death), but the private life insurance was underwritten at time of application.

My boss's friend died in a snowmobiling accident and there was a trace amount of alcohol in his system. The company that provided the private life insurance delivered a cheque in two weeks. The mortgage life insurance claim was denied because one of the exclusions listed in the policy was that coverage would be denied if the insured died in a motorized accident with alcohol present in the bloodstream.

How many people would buy life insurance from an insurance provider that didn't even determine if you qualified for their coverage until after you died?

DON'T SIGN CONTRACTS AT THE DOOR

Someone once told me that years and years ago it was perfectly acceptable to do business at your front door. That must've been a really long time ago. When I hear a knock on the door these days, I fantasize about answering it wearing *Braveheart* face paint while wielding a pitchfork or trident.

Times have certainly changed. Perhaps owing to the previous success of door-to-door sales, it continues in earnest today. And with many door-knockers working on straight commission, you just know some will employ unscrupulous sales tactics from time to time. And because some people who do not have your best interests at heart are sometimes the smoothest operators around, they've effectively ruined it for the few legitimate guys.

This leads me to one of my cardinal rules and I want to be very clear here: *never sign a contract with someone you've never met who shows up unannounced at your door.*

I had a guy show up at our house recently. He insinuated that he was associated with my water company, and offered a free inspection of our water heater. We let him in. Of course, he found lots of potential problems with our existing tank. He made it sound as if it was on the verge of exploding. We wouldn't want the shrapnel piercing the walls and hitting the neighbour's small child, would we? We're rather fond of the neighbours, so we were concerned.

Well, the universe works in funny ways, because he just happened to have a program available that would make it possible to replace our tank with a brand new one, with no cost for the installation and no large, upfront, out-of-pocket costs to us. We just had to pay a monthly rental fee and if anything ever happened to the heater, the company would replace or fix it at no additional cost. It sounded like a fair proposition, assuming that the rental cost, which would include an insurance premium and perhaps a small margin for profit, was not much more expensive than going out and simply replacing the tank with a new unit paid for outright.

It turns out that assumption could not be further from the truth. When the "inspector," who was now revealed to be a salesperson, asked if we were interested, I said no. He asked why, and I replied, "I can do math."

The contract would have locked us in for 15 years, at a total cost to us of $5,545.58. To purchase and install a new tank would cost about $900. In theory, we could buy and install a new water tank every 3 years and still come out ahead. This was a total and utter rip-off. And lots of people have similar stories.

If you're still in doubt, ask any salesperson who comes to your door to leave some literature behind so you can do some digging on your own time. If it's truly a great deal today, it'll be great tomorrow too. If they have the audacity to tell you they have no leave-behind brochures, but they do have legally crafted, 15-page contracts handy, I'd be inclined to chase them down the street with a trident.

If you want to hear me chastise a couple of door-to-door salespeople, download Episode 11 of "Mostly Money, Mostly Canadian" (my podcast on iTunes). Whenever someone comes to my door to sell something, I record the conversation, and if they are bad, I post it. If it saves someone from being duped, then it will have been worth the trouble. These guys were either incompetent, inexperienced, or just shady. Some people said I was too hard on them, but most find the podcast hilarious and informative at the same time. I'll let you be the judge.

The essential message of this chapter is that you need to take the time to read every single word on any document you are thinking of signing. If it would take too long to read before signing, don't sign it on the spot. Take a copy and find the time to read it and understand it. If you can't figure it out, ask a friend, or preferably a lawyer, to help you understand it. No more head-in-the-sand bullshit.

If you've been a follower of my blog, you'll know that I once wrote a post proclaiming Ellen Roseman, personal finance columnist with *The Toronto Star*, to be a saint. She recently penned the book *Fight Back: 81 Ways to Help You Save Money and Protect Yourself from Corporate Trickery*. It is filled with useful information that can help you negotiate lower prices, avoid common pitfalls and traps, and keep more money in your wallet.

CHAPTER FIVE

RULE 5:
DELAY CONSUMPTION

Many people believe that it's too hard to run a surplus. There are just too many demands. It can't be done. They can't even figure out how to run a balanced budget. Their kids need this and that; they have to go on two vacations a year to keep their sanity; they can't make do with a used car—their safety is important so they just have to get the latest SUV, etc.

There are many reasons for this kind of thinking. Three stand out:

1. the keeping-up-with-the-Joneses phenomenon;
2. lifestyle inflation; and
3. the monthly payment trap.

THE KEEPING-UP-WITH-THE-JONESES PHENOMENON

We live to compare. Or perhaps we compare to live. Natural selection dictates that only the fittest survive and so we may be hard-wired to compare ourselves to our peers. If someone buys a fancy new car, perhaps *we* should buy a fancy new car. The problem is that we don't know what that person's finances look like. He or she might be up to their eyeballs in debt, not sleeping at night, and living on a knife's edge. Once you get a fancy new car, after about a month it becomes transportation, just as your old car was. However, it costs more on an ongoing basis. It might attract a few extra glances when you drive around, but who cares?

Well, clearly a lot of us do.

But you can have more than your peers today, or a lot more than your peers tomorrow. By delaying consumption as long as possible, you can build up wealth much more quickly. Suppose you're in the market for a new car. You could afford $800 per month for a fancy German luxury cruiser (that spends 95% of its time taking one person to and from work). Or you could buy a compact car for $200 per month. Insurance will probably be cheaper, and you'll save on gas as well—perhaps another $100 per month in total. Altogether you're saving $700 per month for perhaps 5 years. You could have an all-inclusive trip for two to somewhere tropical once every 3 months, a total of 20 trips, during that same period if you bought the cheaper car. Or you could just put the difference away in a savings account earning 1% interest and have $43,000 after 5 years.

Or consider this: even if you are a car guy (as I am), chances are that 360 days of the year you use your car to simply get you from A to B. Perhaps, at most, you might go for a Sunday drive or a weekend road trip and really want to enjoy the sight and sound and visceral feel of a highly tuned car for a handful of days per year. If that is the case, instead of buying that BMW (or whatever), maybe you should buy a Honda Civic (or whatever) instead. That way you can drive a Ferrari every now and then.

Say what?

Yes, that's right. Let's say you were willing to spend $700 per month more on that BMW, but then decided not to: that works out to $8,400 per year in savings. You could rent a Porsche 911 Cabriolet for eight weekends ($799.95 per weekend + $99.95 insurance + 13% tax at Affinity Luxury Car Rental in Toronto). Or rent a Ferrari 360 Spider for three weekends ($1,999 + $99 insurance + 13% tax, GTAExotics.ca also in Toronto). The best of both worlds would be to rent the exotic car for only one or two weekends to get your fix, and pocket a few grand.

But restraint on spending doesn't have to be limited to cars. One of the biggest expenses (and headaches) you'll have in life can be your home. Some people have a tendency to buy a home based on the most amount of money the bank will lend them. Big mistake. Your goal should be to buy a house that will require the smallest possible mortgage from the bank. The fact that you may not be able to find the perfect house at a lower price range could be an indicator that house prices are too high, or that you're aiming too high. It seems that the days when you lived in a less than ideal house and gradually worked your way up are long gone. Today we see people clamouring to find their "forever house," which has to be perfect and spacious and great for entertaining, etc. But "forever" apparently is about 10 years.

LIFESTYLE INFLATION

Economists keep a close eye on inflation as measured by the consumer price index (CPI). It tells us how much more the stuff we regularly buy costs us over time.

We tend to get pretty worked up about the ever-increasing cost to fill up at the pump—so much so that most people think about various ways to save on gas. What we don't have a good grip on is "lifestyle inflation": the increase in the amount or type of stuff we want to buy over time.

Inflation in prices is something we have no control over as individual consumers. Just ask anyone close to retirement what they paid for their first house and compare that to what they paid for their latest car. My parents' first house in Ottawa was $34,000 in the 1970s and their most recent vehicle purchase was about $40,000. Extrapolate that to when I hit retirement age and a mid-sized sedan might cost $250,000. That's CPI inflation. Lifestyle inflation means that, by then, I'll want a sporty little convertible that could cost $500,000.

Truth serum: I want one of those right now. Really badly. I'm a car guy of the first order, so frivolous spending on all things automotive is high on my want list. I believe that one or two spending vices are okay. It might be travel, sports, home, fashion, or fancy coffee beans. As long as you're not spending beyond your means overall, you can indulge. The problem is that we want to indulge in everything.

As our incomes grow, so do our expenses. You make $30,000 per year, you'll spend $30,000 per year. Fast-forward 10 years and you might be earning $60,000, but spending $60,000. On the lower side of the income spectrum, it's harder to put money aside for savings, because there is a floor of spending required to maintain a basic lifestyle. But everyone has good intentions: we all mean to use our next raise to accelerate debt payments or increase savings, while maintaining our current level of spending. Unfortunately, all too often, the debt payments and savings are not increased but the spending rises.

When a big raise is in the cards, or perhaps a big payment is eliminated, you might ask if now is the time to upgrade your home or cars. "We've got an extra $500 in cash flow. What can we afford to upgrade to now?" The absolute maximum lifestyle inflation you might be able to afford would be to fill that $500 momentary surplus with a new continuing $500 monthly commitment. That would be perennially living at the limit of your means, not within it.

Some of that extra $500 is going to be consumed by CPI inflation. What you are already buying is going to be 2–3% more expensive than last year. The difference between what CPI inflation claims, and what your additional wants claim of that $500 plays a large part in determining how successful you are going to be with your finances. If you don't think seriously about it, you'll discover that every penny of the raise finds a way of getting spent. You'll never get ahead. Too much inflation of either kind is a bad thing. We can't control CPI inflation, but we can control our lifestyle inflation.

Having money doesn't relieve money stress. Spending less than what comes in the door does. This applies to those who make very little, and to those who make a lot.

THE MONTHLY PAYMENT TRAP

More and more people think of big purchases today in terms of monthly payments because we are part of the credit generation. We've been conditioned to finance purchases instead of saving up for them in advance. And it could be one of the main reasons you'll continue to live on the edge with your finances.

The lifetime cost of the interest we pay can be huge. Consider a $30,000 car purchase. If you financed it over 7 years, your total out-of-pocket cost to buy the car would have been just a tick under $35,000 after factoring in the interest. If you had saved up for it in advance, then the out-of-pocket cost was closer to $29,000. That's a $6,000 difference.

I took a look at the same monthly payment for financing the car ($410.06 per month at 4%) and instead put that money into a high-interest savings account to see how long it would take to end up with $30,000. With an interest rate of 1.5%, it would take 5 years and 10 months. If you really do think in terms of monthly payments, then think of this: by financing, you're committed to making that payment for 7 years, whereas you can save the same amount in less than 6 years. If you take a step back and look at the total out-of-pocket cost, it's $34,445.04 to finance (84 months × $410.06) and $28,724.19 to save up in advance (70 months × $410.06).

Of course, in the real world it's not quite that simple. Anyone looking at the above figures would clearly see the benefit of being a saver instead of a borrower. But when you are already spending what's coming in the door (and sometimes more), how do you make that switch? How do you delay purchasing a car for 5 years when you need one today? The answer lies in two underappreciated concepts: discipline and delayed gratification.

It requires hard work and discipline to become more physically fit. The same is true of sorting out our finances. If it was easy, everyone would have an enviable six pack and everyone would have more income than expenses. No one is going to flip the switch for you. You have to want it.

And while there may be some people who really need a new car today, there are many more people who can delay getting a new car for a few years. You could also get a less expensive car for now and put away the monthly difference until you can pay cash for the car you want. There's no law that says your next car always has to be nicer than your last one.

We don't need to limit the conversation to cars. We could be talking about a new stereo, a vacation, or any other big-ticket item. Anything you are financing applies.

The best way to start is to start small. Take baby steps and open up a high-interest savings account with a $50 pre-authorized contribution on the days you get paid. After a few months, if you don't feel a pinch, increase your savings amount until you do. The recipes for physical and financial success are both basic but hard to stick to. No pain, no gain.

Not all debt is the same. Good luck buying your first house with your savings. Ditto for a car. Plus you may have just gone through school, met your future spouse, got married, and had a child. In fact, debt is a necessary evil for younger Canadians. Your education and home are appreciating assets. A car is a depreciating asset, but it could take a while to be able to pay for a reliable car. Beyond these almost inescapable items, you really shouldn't be borrowing money for much else. Certainly not for vacations. Not for gifts. And not for eating out.

WE ALL NEED A HOBBY

Hobbies are supposed to be relaxing, a way to distract yourself from day-to-day stresses and activate a different part of the mind. But they also have a way of bleeding bank accounts. And when people think they have money to burn, which is different from whether they actually *have* money to burn, that bleeding can turn into a gush.

Why do people feel compelled to spend big money on hobbies? Some justify it as one aspect of their work-hard-play-hard philosophy. Others do it because they simply believe that bigger is better. And when it comes to sports, people often link winning with the level of enjoyment they get out of the activity and throw lots of money at top-of-the-line equipment and accessories.

For example, I like to golf, but I wouldn't call myself a golfer. I'm more of an aerator of lawns. The way I see it, I don't need a $400 Tiger Woods Nike driver made out of unobtainium to beat the heck out of the tee box. I do just fine with my no-name clubs.

But I've hit the greens for networking reasons with players who look like they have stepped right off the fairways at the Masters. In the quest to look and play like a pro, they have filled their bags to the brim with the latest clubs and gadgets, such as special golf-course GPS units or laser-based rangefinders. When they took that first swing, though, the jig was up: the thousands of dollars they had spent on tarting up their golf bag did nothing to improve their handicap.

Sometimes it's not how much money you spend on your hobbies, but how you spend it that's the real waste. Auto racing used to be a serious pastime of mine, and the track was littered with drivers who poured thousands of dollars into performance parts to end up only a few tenths of a second per lap faster. Sometimes they were even slower. If they had instead spent a small fraction of those expenses on professional race-driver training, they might have seen an actual improvement in their performance.

Less athletic hobbyists can also fall victim to poor financial trade-offs in the quest to be the best. Take stamp collecting: it takes a lot of money to amass a decent collection. But if you let go of the idea of being at the top of your hobby field, and just enjoy the act itself, it can bring as much pleasure at a much lower cost. A lifelong stamp collector told me that the true joy of collecting comes from the community, the sharing of knowledge, and a common love. The fact is that having a hobby need not be a strain on your bank account— period. The investment of time, which, remember, is free, is all that is needed to ignite the passion. So try to resist the temptation to pour irrational sums of money into your hobby, especially when picking up a new one. Focus instead on that initial investment of time. Once you have a sense of how much pleasure you're actually going to get out of the activity, and how serious a participant you intend to become, you can think about how you want to spend your money.

In the end, your bank account can probably only withstand one serious hobby. If you dump a lot of money into every new activity you try, you will have less to spend on your passion when you do find it.

Thinking of taking up golf? Think twice before buying the best equipment. A big investment can turn into a big waste if you end up not sticking with it. Consider the cost of outfitting yourself with top-of-the-line golf gear:

- Driver: $450
- Fairway wood: $280
- Set of irons: $1,050
- Wedge: $140
- Putter: $300
- Bag: $200
- Golf shoes: $230
- Course-appropriate outfit: $400
- Gloves: $30
- Balls, tees, and miscellaneous: $60
- Total: $3,140 before setting foot on a course

You could instead settle for an entry-level outfit combined with training and green fees on an easy course:

- Complete starter set of clubs, including bag: $250
- Two days of golf school: $500
- Lower-end golf shoes: $100
- Gloves: $30
- Balls, tees, and miscellaneous: $25
- Unlimited season pass to nine-hole course, driving range, chipping and putting greens: $1,000
- Total: $1,905 and you could play all day, the entire season*

LIFESTYLE INFLATION WITH HOUSING

We all know someone who's worn love goggles. They start dating someone new and their whole world starts revolving around that special someone who can do no wrong, even though everyone else seems to think otherwise. Once the honeymoon phase is over,

---

*All prices before taxes. Golf school and training academy membership rates quoted by Deer Creek Academy in Ontario at time of writing. Prices may have changed.

the goggles come off, a dramatic breakup ensues, and suddenly everything seems so clear. "Why didn't you guys say anything?" the friend asks. Human psychology is a powerful force.

Meet Ben Rabidoux. He's a friend who has been trying to warn Canadians about the love affair we have with home ownership. Mr. Rabidoux is the president of North Cove Advisors, Inc., which is a market research firm covering Canadian macroeconomics, housing, and credit for institutional investors. His website, TheEconomicAnalyst.com, provides easy-to-digest graphs that essentially explain themselves, but he also weaves together ideas that combine to reveal a sobering new reality we may soon be facing. Already offended by the premise? He's used to it.

Here are a few pieces of hard data from his site: in 1975, the average size of a house in Canada was 1,050 square feet. Fast-forward to 2010 and newly built homes almost doubled in size to an average of 1,950 square feet. This increase has been accompanied by a decrease in the average number of people living in a household. In 1971, it was 3.5; by 2006, that number had fallen by a full person to 2.5.

Whereas in 1999 the price of a home was 3.2 times income, this multiple had ballooned to 5.9 times income in 2010. Essentially, the amount of money we are willing to pay for a house has increased much faster than our incomes. Instead of buying beer, we've switched to champagne, but we still can afford only beer. That's some serious lifestyle inflation.

RENOVATING IS AN INVESTMENT?

We are the generation of the renovation. Granite countertop upgrades, hardwood floor installations, take a wall down here, feng shui there, etc. There are so many shows on TV centred around renovation that you might start to feel abnormal if you aren't refurbishing your home. Then again, with so many people living at or beyond their means, why would you want to be normal?

There are two main reasons why you would undertake home renovations. The first is because you want to improve your living space. The second is the belief that you are making an investment that will increase the value of your home more than the cost of making the changes. My beef is with the people who use the second reason to justify their financial irresponsibility.

Don't get me wrong, I don't have anything against upgrading your living space—even if you don't get a positive return on investment. You just have to be able to afford it. (And it would be nice if it didn't end your relationship with your significant other too!)

Let's say your $50,000 renovation increases the value of your home by $75,000. That's a total return of 50% on your investment. That's great if you're a flipper, but what if you live in that home for another 10 years? Your annualized rate of return is only 4.14% if there is no change in the overall value of your property in those 10 years (which can happen), and that assumes the upgrade is as desirable 10 years from now as it is today. It doesn't factor in the increase in price of the property, but keep in mind that properties can have negative growth over 10 years too. You are also forgoing the use of that $50,000. If you borrow it, your cash flow is tied up paying it off. If you paid for it in cash, you have to weigh the opportunity cost of other investments.

So, as I said, I don't care if you renovate. Your new environment may bring you great pleasure and pride. And that's wonderful. There are also many renovations that make great investments. If you can afford it, go nuts. If it puts a strain on your finances though, don't fall into the trap of justifying because it's an investment.

Listen, I'll be the first person to tell you that I'm not normal, but I really dislike most renovations. Not because they don't make a house prettier or more functional: it's fun to see the before and after pictures of a reno. I get a kick out of seeing body transformations from people who start a new diet or exercise plan too. The problem I have is that one of these things is a true investment, and while the other is often justified as one, it is really nothing more than conspicuous consumption.

Eating better and getting proper exercise is an investment in your health. It doesn't have to cost much either. A friend of mine recently showed me his rock-hard six-pack abs, which *Jersey Shore*'s "The Situation" would envy. His entire workout routine requires a chin-up bar ($50) and two chairs. He started out more like the rest of us, with a midsection another friend described as "The Predicament." This is the kind of investment I like to see: low investment, great return.

Renovations are a different kettle of fish. I'm well aware of projects that can increase the value of a house, and flippers can make a comfortable living by finding hidden gems and quickly turning them around for a substantial profit. But let's be serious. Many home renovations are falsely justified as a long-term investment. The justification helps some people rationalize their urge to spend and consume. And upgrade.

If you have the money in hand, and your finances are in order, I'll be the first person to tell you that if you want to build a staircase made of ivory (synthetic, natch), then be my guest. I couldn't care less what floats your boat when you can afford it. The problem is that many people can't afford it. They finance it instead. And here is where it gets tricky. Borrowing money to invest is speculative. If you do the same thing in the stock market, you're immediately assumed to be in the medium-high-to-totally-bonkers category with respect to your appetite for risk. The amount of paperwork you have to sign to acknowledge the risk is cumbersome because financial institutions want to cover their butts if things go sour.

Borrowing to invest in a home reno is different. You can enjoy tangible benefits right away. Your house is easier on the eyes and more functional. It makes you feel good. Perhaps you've one-upped your friends. Now you're the ones with a "situation" and they're the ones with a "predicament." But the investment works out, psychologically at least, because we're in what may be the longest secular bull market in real estate history in Canada, and enjoying 30 years of falling interest rates. If the housing market doesn't change, we could easily tease out the value of renovations by seeing how much more you sell your house for than you paid for it. If the increase is more than the cost of the reno, it's a profitable investment. But the housing market is dynamic: it doesn't go up forever, no matter what the current trends are, and you might find that one day the overall decline in the value of the house is more than the increase attributed to a reno.

This is the point at which people chime in to say that the reno was for themselves, not an investment. And this is where I say, yes, that was the real reason all along, and if you financed it over many years, then you couldn't afford it. It was just conspicuous consumption.

Guess what? We've covered everything you need to know to be financially better off than most people. As I said at the beginning of this book, the rules are not hard to understand, but they are hard to implement.

Once you've mastered them, then you can go on and pursue that A+ in personal finance. You can do that by reading more books (and I'll provide the titles of a few more to consider in Part 2). You can manage things on your own, or you can find an advisor. (In fact, I believe the vast majority of people need an advisor, so I'll provide some tips on how to find a good one.)

And you can also always check with me for general guidance. Follow me on Twitter (@preetbanerjee) and I'm more than happy to answer any questions you might have.

PART 2
BEYOND THE FIVE RULES

You've been waiting long enough to read about investing, so I'll start Part 2 with that.

Whether you want to use an advisor or not, the principles of prudent investing are the same. You can save yourself a lot of money over your lifetime if you do it yourself, but if you make a few simple, easily made mistakes, you can end up costing yourself a lot more in lost performance than what you save in fees.

These are heated discussions among investor advocates, DIY investors, and the financial services industry, but they are of little consequence for those just starting out: how much you contribute to your portfolio in the beginning is far more important than pretty much anything else.

Remember the example I offered in the introduction: put $200 per month into a high-interest savings account that pays a measly 1.5% and you'll have almost $26,000 after 10 years. Invest just $100 per month and to make the same kind of money, an amount just shy of $26,000, you'll need an annualized return of more than 14% on your portfolio. So even if you use a financial advisor who puts your savings in relatively high-fee funds, you'll be fine if you just focus on putting money away. Once your portfolio gets to the $50,000 mark, not only will you have more options when it comes to dealing with advisors, you also will have reached the point at which you can start to benefit from more advanced concepts, such as fees. Until then, don't over-think it. Just put money away and learn the basics of investing to make sure you aren't dealing with a particularly bad advisor.

After we've covered what you need to know about investing, we can tackle the value of financial advisors. The average Canadian will end up using one, and the average, supposedly savvy Canadian has a very polarized opinion about them: they tend to either love financial advisors or hate them. I'm going to show you how to use one effectively, and how to pick them in the first place. But remember, you shouldn't worry too much about this in the beginning. You've got time to figure it out before it really matters. I can almost guarantee that your first financial advisor won't be your last one anyway.

We'll also take a more in-depth look at life insurance, including how to figure out how much you need. At the very least, by the end of the book, you'll be speaking a bit of the same language as your agent, which helps you to make a more informed decision about something so critical.

CHAPTER SIX

INVESTING BASICS

I'll cut to the chase now, and then I'll explain why it's the best way to go.

When it comes to investing, you want to use what is called a "portfolio fund." These are turnkey investment portfolios that don't require much monitoring at all. They will incorporate all the prudent ingredients of a proper portfolio and do all the work for you. All you have to do is add money and wait.

I use a turnkey portfolio fund for the majority of my investing. I know a lot about investing: I've even ghost-written an entire book explaining advanced investment techniques for a large financial advisory firm in the United States. The book was distributed to their financial advisors, but essentially all the techniques described in it are available in turnkey portfolio funds. For multi-million-dollar portfolios, investors who are paying lots of money to financial advisors need to see that something is being done for the money they pay, so instead of using a turnkey portfolio, they generally build the same overall portfolios using individual building blocks. It makes rich people feel special. The relative costs might be lower, but that's partly due to the economies of scale.

So when it comes to your investing, do what I do. If it's a portfolio fund that invests in stocks and bonds, both here and around the world, and it balances itself, go for it. When you are starting out, the fees aren't that important. Once your portfolio gets to about $50,000, reach out to me on Twitter (@preetbanerjee) and I'll tell you what to look at next. For the record, I don't manage people's money anymore, so I don't receive any compensation for my recommendations.

In the meantime, in order to work with an advisor (or to become a do-it-yourself investor eventually), you need to speak the language. Let's look at the basics of what you should know.

RISK AND RETURN

Ask someone who doesn't know a lick about investing to recite an investing buzzword or phrase, and "risk and return" may be among the first responses. But what does it mean?

The phrase refers to the notion that higher returns come with higher risk. Risk, bluntly, is what you can lose. When you start looking at the A+ material on risk, you'll see that risk is used to describe how much volatility your portfolio experiences, or how much it goes up and down, assuming you have a properly diversified portfolio.

But what you need to know now is that taking on higher risk does not mean you automatically get higher returns. It means you have the *potential* for higher returns. You could take on more risk and end up with lower returns, or negative returns, or even lose all your money in extreme cases. If investors are willing to take on risk, it is only rational for them to expect to be compensated through a higher potential return on their investment.

The greater the potential return, the greater the risk. This is a fundamental relationship. However, it should also be noted that the relationship is not linear. Rather, for every extra unit of potential return you desire, you should expect a disproportionately greater amount of extra risk: risk grows exponentially with potential return. Figure 6.1 illustrates the relationship.

From a 30,000-foot perspective, cash (in the form of a high-interest savings account or guaranteed investment certificate) is essentially risk-free. But low risk also comes with the guarantee of low returns.

**Figure 6.1: Risk grows exponentially
with potential return on investment**

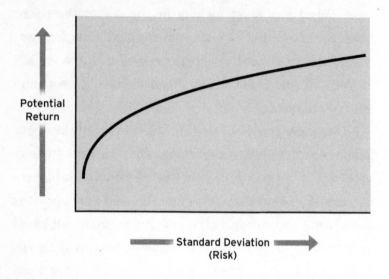

Potential
Return

Standard Deviation
(Risk)

Right now, cash investments are paying about 1%, but
you know you'll get your 1% consistently.

The *long-term* average return is greater on investments that promise higher returns, but so is the range
of returns, and so is the risk. If you buy one single stock,
it's possible to more than double your money (a 100%
or greater return) or lose all of your money (a negative
100% return).

DIVERSIFICATION

The term "diversification" is routinely used to mean not putting all your eggs in one basket, in order to reduce risk. If you have six eggs all in a basket and you drop that basket, all your eggs are ruined. But if each egg has its own basket, then your chances of dropping and destroying all your eggs declines dramatically.

Consider the investor who purchases shares in only one stock. If the stock doubles in value, the investor is delighted that he or she has earned a 100% rate of return. If, on the other hand, the company goes bankrupt, the investor loses 100% of his or her original investment. If the investor instead purchases shares in 100 different companies in equal dollar amounts, then the effect of one company going bankrupt would be to reduce the portfolio's total value by no more than 1%. If one company doubles in value, it similarly produces only a 1% increase in the value of the portfolio. Of course, the prudent goal would be to pick 100 companies that each represent a solid long-term investment. While one or two may become bankrupt, one or two are likely to double or triple in value and perhaps the majority will yield an average of 6–8% over the long term.

Diversification can reduce risk, but it can't eliminate it. There is a certain amount of risk in any market that can't be diversified away. Think about what happens if an economy is heading into a recession. There is a tendency for everything to go down because people have less money to spend on everything they usually spend money on.

STOCKS VERSUS BONDS VERSUS CASH

There is no rule that says a portfolio can only be made up of stocks. You can also own bonds and cash. There are other options as well, but these are the big three you'll need to worry about for now. So what's the difference?

Stocks are commonly called "equities" because they represent ownership, or equity, in a company. They tend to be more volatile in price, and over the very long run, stock markets are expected to have higher returns than bond markets and cash. They are therefore expected to be much riskier. A portfolio made up entirely of stocks can lose 30% or more of its value in a year. It can also gain 30% or more. On average, stocks are expected to return 6–8% over very long periods, but the ride can be extremely unnerving.

Bonds are commonly referred to as "fixed income," because they pay a set amount on a fixed schedule. If stocks represent ownership, bonds represent a loan to a company. If you buy a bond for $1,000, it's as if you are lending out $1,000. Until you get it back, you get interest payments of a fixed amount, on fixed dates. Bonds can fluctuate in price, and not all loans are good ones. Having said that, bonds, or fixed income investments, are considered to be less risky than stocks overall. They can still lose money in a given year, but the range of possible returns is generally muted compared to stocks.

Cash is considered risk-free. It won't lose money, but it won't gain much either. Low risk, low return. The cash component of a portfolio can be in the form of money in a high-interest savings account, GICs, and less ideally these days, in a money market mutual fund.

Very few portfolios are 100% allocated to any one of these categories. Typically, you might see a mix like this: 55% invested in equities (stocks), 40% in fixed income (bonds), and 5% in cash.

ASSET ALLOCATION

An "asset class" can be defined as a group of securities that tend to behave in a similar fashion relative to one another—and are constructed and regulated according to a common set of rules. So stocks, fixed income, and cash all can be considered asset classes. Asset allocation is the actual distribution of money across different asset classes.

I've already suggested what a typical portfolio allocation might look like, but there are a number of possibilities. For example, you might have 70% of your portfolio in equities, 30% in fixed income, and no money allocated to cash. Equities, fixed income, and cash are the asset classes and, in this case, 70/30/0% is the asset allocation. When an asset allocation does not include an allocation to cash (as is often the case), 70/30/0% is usually referred to as simply 70/30%.

One of the fundamental assumptions of asset allocation is that the best-performing asset class changes from year to year and there is no reliable predictive tool for determining ahead of time which asset class will be the best performer. Therefore, combining asset classes is a prudent strategy to reduce the overall risk of the portfolio. Often, if stocks are going down, bonds might be going up. But note that it's possible for stocks and bonds to go down in value at the same time too. Both asset classes are expected to go up over the very long term, but each class has its own cycle.

The more stocks you have in your portfolio (as a percentage of the overall portfolio), the more volatile your portfolio will be. The more fixed income you have in your portfolio, the less volatile it will be. But because stocks have historically outperformed bonds, people often weight their portfolio too heavily in stocks, hoping to get their money to grow faster. They think they understand that the increased risk means a bumpier ride, and they think they can ride out the storms. But when the storms come, they often quickly find out they can't.

Generally speaking, people put too much equity in their portfolio. A useful rule of thumb is that your age should be your percentage allocation to fixed income. So if you are 30 years old, you should have 30% fixed income, and therefore 70% equity. If you are 50 years old, you should have 50% fixed income and 50% equity, and if you are 65, you would have 65% fixed income and 35% equity. This is not a bad rule, and it's in line with the overall theme of this book, which is to not over-think things. Just set your portfolio's allocation to fixed income to be as close as possible to your age. I say "as close as possible" because many investment firms will have a set of turnkey portfolios with set allocations. For example, they might have conservative, moderate, and aggressive options, which are 35/65%, 60/40%, and 75/25%, respectively (the first figure in each case representing the percentage in stocks). Just pick the one that comes closest to following the rule.

REBALANCING

Since different asset classes are expected to conform to different patterns, it is possible and probable that the target asset allocation will be violated through the normal-course market movements. On a broad level, if the portfolio has a 50% weighting to equities and 50% to fixed income, and through normal market movements stocks go on a bull run and increase by 20% while bonds are flat, then the portfolio will drift to an allocation closer to 60% equities and 40% bonds. A portfolio with an asset mix of 50/50% will have less risk than a portfolio with an asset mix of 60/40%, so it's necessary to bring the portfolio's overall asset allocation back in line with the original allocation.

There is a double-edged ancillary effect to rebalancing because portfolio return variance can be reduced while long-term returns may be either increased *or* decreased. By rebalancing back from 60/40% to 50/50%, you are, in essence, buying low and selling high.

Take the case where stocks run up 20% in short order: by selling off a portion of the equities to bring back the allocation to 50% equities and 50% fixed income, you are selling stocks at a potential high. A portion of the proceeds are then used to purchase additional bonds, which are at a potential low, because they're flat and the expected long-term performance of bonds is net positive. So constant rebalancing reduces the return variance of the portfolio. However, it also is possible that you are selling the stocks before their bull run is over. In this case, less of your portfolio is subject to the exceptional performance that could be afforded by a bull run in stocks resulting in a lower potential return for the portfolio overall. Rebalancing too frequently reduces long-term portfolio return, while rebalancing too infrequently increases the portfolio return variance. Therefore, the goal of rebalancing is to find a strategy that finds an appropriate balance of these two opposing forces.

Once again, if you simply follow the investing recommendations later in this section, you won't have to worry about rebalancing. Nonetheless, the information is presented here in case you opt to use a different strategy.

RISK-PROFILE QUESTIONNAIRES

A risk-profile questionnaire is a simple tool designed to find the right asset allocation for your portfolio. It generally consists of 10–15 simple multiple-choice questions. If you answer the questions and your score is indicative of someone who doesn't like risk, the asset allocation recommendation is going to be weighted more heavily in fixed income and cash than equities.

Conversely, if your score shows you have a high tolerance for risk, your recommended asset allocation might be more heavily weighted to stocks. That means you can expect high risk and the potential of high returns, but the possibility of high losses as well, especially over the short term.

Risk-profile questionnaires are ubiquitous with investment transactions in Canada, but they've come under heavy criticism in some quarters. Do we put too much "stock" in them? Or are they just not good enough?

It would be hard to meet with an investor today who hasn't completed a risk-profile questionnaire. But given how often investors switch gears with their investment strategies, largely because of their inability to stomach risk, it seems that the questionnaires are ineffective. President of the Investor Education Fund (IEF.ca) Tom Hamza notes that there are two levels of risk: "Actual investment risk, and the risk that comes from not knowing about what you are investing in. Actual investment risk is magnified if you don't understand the basics of the products that you are investing in. We see a lot of people magnify the first risk with the second because they haven't taken the time to understand their investments."

Anecdotally, financial advisors note that sometimes investors answer the questions as if they are taking a test. They select the answers they think a successful investor would choose instead of those that reflect what they really feel. For example, a staple question is about the degree of loss in a given year you could tolerate before feeling uncomfortable. The possible responses range from none to moderate double-digit-percentage losses. Some might be inclined to select the highest degree of loss because they've seen some compelling statistics about the virtue of holding tight through the bad times and the trade-off between risk and potential return. Taking on the risk an aggressive investor is comfortable with when you are actually a conservative investor is a tall order.

The fact that many of these questionnaires are completed in under 5 minutes should be enough of a clue that they aren't sufficiently nuanced to form the basis for long-term investment decisions. Some can be completed in under 60 seconds. These assessments, at best, should be used as one of many different tools when assessing the risk tolerance of an investor.

Imagine filling in a 5-minute questionnaire about a prospective spouse as the sole criterion for spending a life together. Sure, we all have boxes that need to be ticked off when it comes to what we are or are not looking for, but there's obviously much more to it. The next time you are presented with a risk-profile questionnaire, it should be accompanied by a lengthy discussion about risk. Otherwise, the results are worth the time you put into it, which is very little.

TIME HORIZON

They say it's "time in the market" and not "timing the market" that breeds the most successful investors. Over the short term, it's impossible to know what your returns will be like. Over the long term, the probability of a positive return and for stocks to outperform bonds, which will outperform cash, is greater. But how long is long?

Long Term Is 10 Years or More

In a recent academic paper, "Investing for the Long Run," a long-term investor is described as someone with little or no specific short-term liabilities or demands for liquidity relative to the amount of capital invested.* Translation for retail investors: you shouldn't need to touch the money in your portfolio for at least 10 years. One of the main advantages of having a 10-year investment horizon, according to the authors, is that long-term investors have the ability to ride out

---

* Andrew Ang and Knut N. Kjaer, "Investing for the Long Run" (November 11, 2011). Available at SSRN: http://ssrn.com/abstract=1958258 or http://dx.doi.org/10.2139/ssrn.1958258

short-term fluctuations. Well, in theory, that's one of the advantages. In practice, it can be very difficult to keep your cool when stock market returns make the headlines on a daily basis.

A prudent long-term portfolio has a few simple rules:

1. Ensure you have multi-level diversification.
2. Rebalance when necessary.
3. Don't take on risk you can't stomach.
4. Keep fees low.

Multi-level diversification means you diversify not only by holding many securities within the same asset class, but also many different asset classes. But as simple as that sounds, even professionals often can't stick to the plan. The California Public Employees' Retirement System (CalPERS), one of the largest pension funds in the world, had an exposure to equities of 70% of its portfolio in 2007. One year later, market performance brought that allocation down to 52%. CalPERS then sold off equities in the portfolio to bring the allocation even lower, to 44%. They changed their strategy mid-swing. They panicked.

In 2008 they sold a $370 million stake in Apple. Had they held onto it, it would be worth around $900 million at the time of writing. That increase would be even greater if they had rebalanced back to the original plan, which would have entailed buying more stock, not selling it.

It should be no surprise to learn that CalPERS has a new chief investment officer. If you've been making changes to your investment strategy on the fly, it might not be the plan that's not working. It might be you not working the plan.

Short Term Is 5 Years or Less

Any money you need to withdraw within 5 years should be in cash or GICs. The short-term performance of stocks and bonds within a 5-year period is too unpredictable. The last thing you want is to have less money to spend than you originally planned. In other words, if you need the money in 5 years or less, keep it away from the stock market.

That leaves us with the medium term, a time horizon between 5 and 10 years. In this case, you can split the difference. If your long-term risk profile suggests you can handle 70% equities and 30% fixed income, cut the equity allocation in half to 35%. Your portfolio allocation should now be 35% equity and 65% fixed income.

Most risk-profile questionnaires ask you about your time horizon and then use that information to make an asset allocation recommendation. But risk-profile questionnaires are all too aggressive in their recommendations. The aggression doesn't matter when markets are strong because returns are turbocharged, but after the credit crisis and market meltdown in 2008, it became apparent that a lot of people can't stomach as much risk as they thought they could. The experience led them to bail out of their investment portfolios at the worst time possible—after they had fallen in value.

It's buy low, sell high, remember?

ACTIVE OR PASSIVE MANAGEMENT (TO START)?

Here's a crash course in active versus passive investment management. I hemmed and hawed about including it, but it's been a hot topic in many books and newspapers, so I thought I would acknowledge that. But I'll do what I've done throughout this book and just give it to you straight. You are better off with passive management (also known as indexing); however, finding an advisor who provides passive management when you don't have a big portfolio is difficult. Luckily, when your portfolio is small, the difference between active and passive management matters less than it will later, when your portfolio has grown. Active investment management involves trying to beat the market. Passive investment management simply tries to replicate the market. Because active management requires the skill of an investment professional who analyzes what investments to make, it costs money. The analyst's team of research associates cost money, too. Passive investment management has no manager: a computer could literally manage the portfolio because all it has to do is hold the same stocks that the market holds in the same proportions. Now, if you take all the active investors in the world and put them together, they collectively get the market return because they, in fact, make up the market. So if the market returns 5% this year, some of those investors made 7%, and some made 3%, but on average they collectively earned 5%, *before costs*.

All the passive investors also earned the market return. Since they weren't trying to beat the market, but rather just do what the market did, every single one of them earned the market return of 5%, *before costs*.

Passive investing costs less than active investing, so *after costs* the passively invested dollar must beat the average actively invested dollar. Every investment firm and every financial advisor will try to tell you that *their* active manager is more astute than everyone else's, but the truth is that there is no way to identify who will outperform the market going forward. For years and years, thousands of doctoral candidates have been trying to identify a reliable predictor of future investment performance. Their collective efforts have yielded no results. In fact, mutual fund companies are required to put a disclaimer on any advertisements that boast about their past performance reporting to indicate that "past performance may not be repeated."

Because of all of this, most people are better off in a low-cost, passively managed portfolio. You might get a better return with an actively managed fund, but chances are you won't. This hard truth has been proven time and time again by academics with no bias and without deep pockets. Unfortunately, the industry with lots of bias (they make a lot of money selling actively managed investments), and incredibly deep pockets, will do anything to convince you otherwise.

The good news is that it doesn't matter if you're just starting out. The differences are inconsequential. Over time they add up, but you've got time to do your homework and make up your own mind.

Let's assume you have $100 per month to contribute. If the market return is 7% for the next 5 years, then an actively managed portfolio fund that pays a financial advisor a fee might cost you 2.50% per year, meaning the return your money earns is 4.5%. On the other hand, a passively managed portfolio fund with no advisor to pay might have a fee of 1.0%, so its return is 6%. If we fast-forward 5 years, the more expensive, actively managed portfolio fund is now worth $6,714.56. The passively managed portfolio fund is worth $6,977.00. After 5 years, the difference is $262.45. If you're getting assistance from a financial advisor, the extra $262.45 over those 5 years could be a bargain. If we keep fast-forwarding, however, after 40 years the actively managed portfolio grows to $134,115.07, while the passively managed portfolio grows to $199,149—a difference of more than $65,000. So at some point, you'll want to address costs, but it's not critical over the first few years, assuming that you're building up your portfolio slowly. It's more important to get going.

If you want to learn more about low-cost, DIY investment portfolios, I recommend *The MoneySense Guide to the Perfect Portfolio* by Dan Bortolotti. Dan is also the author of the brilliant blog CanadianCouchPotato.com, which focuses on index investing for Canadians.

WHAT TO INVEST IN

If you want the least amount of hassle, do the following for any portfolio you aren't planning to touch for at least 10 years: set your target fixed income allocation to your age. So if you are 30, you'll have 30% in fixed income and 70% in equities. Next, you'll want a turnkey portfolio mutual fund. This is a fund made up of several underlying funds that have been strategically placed together to create a diversified portfolio. It will have exposure to stocks and bonds from around the world. It will also automatically rebalance. All you have to do is add money to it. You can do this either with an advisor, or by yourself.

If you use an advisor, chances are you will be given a questionnaire to fill out. If you have a small portfolio, or are starting one for the first time, the advisor is most likely going to offer you a portfolio fund of some sort that has relatively high fees and penalties for leaving. That's okay for now.

For example, the fund might have a management expense ratio (MER) of 2.5%, which means 2.5% of the value of the fund is deducted for fees every year. You won't see it happen, it just happens. There might be a penalty of 5% (which you *will* see) if you take your money out within the first few years (see the section on mutual fund compensation in Chapter 7 for more details). All of this gets lots of attention from investor advocates, but if you're investing only $100 per month, you're looking at roughly $15 in fees over the first year, and $45 for year two. At the end of the second year, you would have contributed $2,400 and if you needed to withdraw it all for an emergency you could pay a redemption fee of $120.

Are these fees relatively high? Yes. Are they absolutely high? A fee of $180 for financial planning assistance is a bargain. A fee of $180 for nothing but investment advice is stiff.

If you feel you can set up a mindless portfolio fund on your own (anyone can really), my first choice for a new investor is one of ING Direct Canada's Streetwise funds (check for their new name in 2014). These funds have an MER of 1.07% and are butt-simple to set up and maintain. Until you get a more sizeable portfolio, and until you get to an A+ with investment portfolios, these funds are fine. (Full disclosure: I have consulted for ING Direct Canada in the past, and there is a reasonable expectation that I will do so in the future.)

The account-opening process will contain a simple risk-profile questionnaire. If the recommended portfolio fund is within one notch of your target asset allocation, you're good to go. If it's way off, err on the side of caution and pick the fund with the lowest risk (weighted most heavily to fixed income) between the two options. To change your selected fund, you just have to go back and adjust your answers on the risk-profile questionnaire to be less risk-seeking. It will give you a less risky fund to invest in once you change your answers.

I realize that they've put together their questions based on industry research, but the entire industry must use the same consultants because the various risk-profile questionnaires out there all are similarly too aggressive in their recommendations. The proof of the pudding is in the eating. People bailed on their recommended portfolios en masse during the credit crisis. That should be enough for the industry to realize the questionnaires aren't good enough, but not much has changed since.

TO DIY OR NOT TO DIY

A friend once asked me about dumping his financial advisor so he could save money on fees. He said he had been seeing a lot of positive mentions of low-cost index funds and wondered if that was the way to go. It is true that index funds are appealing for various reasons: they have lower costs because you don't have to pay for a star fund manager and his or her staff of researchers. They also are tax-efficient because the portfolio doesn't get tinkered with a lot, and so on. There is no shortage of proponents of index investing. But what does using or not using an advisor have to do with active versus passive investment strategies? Not much, as it turns out.

I believe my friend assumed that financial advice comes at a high price, and do-it-yourself investing is cheap. That's a one-dimensional way of looking at things. If instead we look at it from a two-dimensional perspective, we can plot the pros and cons on an advice-or-no-advice axis, and an active-or-passive-management axis. Now we have four broad conditions: DIY with passive strategies; DIY with active strategies; use an advisor with passive strategies; and use an advisor with active strategies. In the real world, there are many more possibilities, such as investors who use an advisor for the bulk of their portfolio and manage their own smaller account as well. Both portfolios could involve a blend of active and passive strategies.

And here's the kicker. It's quite possible that an investor using active management through an advisor can end up better off at the end of the day than a DIY investor using a passive strategy. (It's also not always a given that the active-advisor route is the most expensive after calculating exchange-traded fund commissions for some DIY investors. I've seen some pretty active DIY accounts using passive products, and this qualifies as active management.) Once you factor in the ancillary planning expertise of a good advisor, which might encompass tax planning, estate planning, insurance planning, and much more, the average 1% fee for advice can be a bargain.

But it's not always about cost.

Many DIY investors have explained to me that they decided to take their finances completely into their own hands, mostly because of some level of frustration with the returns they were getting. Maybe they felt they were being gouged, or they were sick of their advisor hiding when the markets turned south, and perhaps they just felt that every phone call or meeting was attached to a sales pitch of some sort.

I'm a big fan of DIY investing, but I'm also a fan of advice and financial planning. I think most people would agree that good advice is hard to find, and therein lies a large part of the problem. We don't mind paying a bit more when we feel we are getting value for our money.

In addition to the apparent savings, one of the other major reasons people take up DIY investing is that the barriers are very low. A few mouse clicks and you can carry out your own trades.

Contrast the predicament of an individual who is looking for a financial advisor and one who is looking for, say, a builder. If you hire a contractor to fix the foundation of your house and they're too slow, expensive, or unprofessional, you might fire them and have someone else take over. If that second contractor is similarly inept, you would probably suck it up and invest a lot more time finding a third contractor, whom you would vet much more carefully. You would persist in searching for a third party to handle the project because it's clearly a large undertaking due to the physical, equipment, and time requirements. You're not likely to attempt it yourself. But when it comes to investing, the DIY option appears to be more manageable. Certainly, there are DIY investors who have learned the ropes out of sheer frustration, and manage quite well. They may hire a fee-only advisor to help with a financial plan for the less sexy estate, tax, and retirement planning.

Some people constantly switch strategies and end up with a hodgepodge of investments, with no regard for the overall portfolio construction. And then, of course, there are those who buy high and panic when markets dip and then sell low and lose much more money than mutual funds with the highest fees would cost them. Not that I'm recommending that you invest in high-fee mutual funds, mind you.

What I would suggest is to take the time to figure out what makes a good advisor a good advisor. That's more than just checking to see if they're a certified financial planner (CFP) or possess one of the myriad other credentials out there. You need to roll up your sleeves and invest some time to learn at least the basics of their lingo, the basics of the "cost matters hypothesis,"* diversification, how advisors get paid, portfolio construction, and more.

---

* The cost matters hypothesis essentially states that the higher the fees (the cost of financial intermediation), the lower the returns of the investors as a group.

If you can learn the language your advisor speaks, you will be better able to find one of the good ones and determine the value you are receiving for the extra cost.

RRSP OR TFSA?

You would have to have been living under a rock if you haven't heard of registered retirement savings plans (RRSPs). But then, financially speaking, many people do live under rocks.

Many people equate RRSPs to—drum roll, please!—retirement planning. They've been around for a long time (since 1957) and, until recently, have been the de facto method of saving for retirement, besides, or in addition to, pension plans.

Things got much more complicated when tax-free savings accounts (TFSAs) were introduced. Many people are now opting to save into a TFSA instead of an RRSP for their retirement. Others are using a mix of both. These two tax-sheltered accounts are similar, but there are nuanced differences between them. Let's start by looking at RRSPs.

Many people think that they buy RRSPs every year—that the RRSP is the investment. No. Think of an RRSP as an account. You can hold a wide variety of investments inside this account. An RRSP can be set up as a high-interest savings account or a guaranteed investment certificate. It can hold stocks, bonds, and mutual funds, or it can hold a combination of these different options.

The reason many Canadians save into an RRSP is because they are tempted by the dangling carrot of a tax refund. You know that if you earn $100, part of that goes to the government in the form of income tax. But, up to certain limits, money put into your RRSP isn't subject to income tax. Now, what normally happens is that you get paid, and taxes are taken out of your pay at source, before you have access to your money. Let's say you made $50,000 before tax. You might pay $10,000 in income tax, which is taken off your paycheque. But if you put $1,000 into an RRSP account over the year, in the eyes of the government, you only have to pay the income tax owed by someone who earned $49,000. Since you paid the tax a $50,000-earner was supposed to pay, but are only supposed to have paid the tax a $49,000-earner was supposed to pay, you get back the difference at tax time.

Sounds great, right? Well, not so fast. Eventually, the piper has to get paid. The trade-off is that when you take money out of your RRSP account in the future, it gets treated as salaried income, meaning it is subject to tax. So an RRSP is a giant tax-deferral mechanism. While you are deferring income tax, you hope to grow your savings by investing it as you (or your advisor) sees fit.

Another benefit of an RRSP is that many Canadians will be in a lower tax bracket in retirement than they were in their working years. That means you save paying tax at a higher rate when contributing to an RRSP and end up owing tax at a lower rate when taking it back out. For these basic reasons, coupled with the length of time that the RRSP program has been around, it's a very popular savings (and investing) option for Canadians.

A few years ago, the government introduced the tax-free savings account (TFSA). The account was originally designed as a short- to medium-term savings plan, but due to its structure, has become a very popular retirement savings vehicle as well. Let's look at how it works.

It's almost exactly the same as an RRSP—with this big difference: you don't get any tax savings upfront, and you don't have to pay any tax down the road when you take funds out. So what's all the hoopla about? Well, to a certain extent, there's just a lot of hair-splitting going on. Everybody's financial situation is different. To make a long story short, there are so many variables at play in determining which plan or account is better for you that there is no clear winner.

At least not in a way that can be recommended for everyone. Just Google "RRSP versus TFSA" and you'll see there is no straight answer.

So here is what you need to know if you are just starting out. If you use an advisor, do what he or she says. If you aren't using an advisor, use the TFSA first. Don't over-think it. The differences are too close to call and all the variables that affect the calculations are constantly changing. The RRSP versus TFSA analysis is an A+ discussion. The easy A is just having a long-term savings account. Focus on having savings for the long term and you're beating the majority of Canadians out there.

One place to look for a great analysis of the RRSP-versus-TFSA debate is in *The Wealthy Barber Returns* by David Chilton. His first book, *The Wealthy Barber*, is one of the most famous books in Canada. Not just for personal finance, but for any type of book, period. His latest effort offers up a number of valuable financial lessons on a variety of topics and is definitely on my recommended list.

CHAPTER SEVEN

FINANCIAL ADVISORS

While many people are capable of handling their own investment portfolios (see Chapter 6), most of those same people are neither as capable, nor as interested, in handling their overall financial planning. For those who take a keen interest in personal finance (but focus mostly on investing), there is a sharp division between the camp that thinks financial advisors are a waste of time and the one that doesn't.

For the most part, the arguments against consulting a financial advisor are to the effect that they are not sufficiently well trained, that they are commission-hungry salespeople who don't always put their clients' interests ahead of their own, and that investors would be better off without them to save on cost. It's difficult to argue against those points en masse, but in spite of that, I believe most Canadians would be better off with a financial advisor. They just need to find a good one.

I have been one of the loudest proponents of the first two criticisms. It only takes a few weeks of self-study to pass an exam that lets you sell mutual funds to Canadians, so it's no surprise that there are some less-than-competent financial advisors out there. There are, however, many advisors who continue to study for years and are very sharp indeed. The flaw in the way many people look at financial advisors is similar to what I pointed out at the beginning of this book. If you're going to a financial advisor solely for investment advice, you're doing it wrong. The value of the advice lies in its comprehensiveness.

Whether or not you want to go it alone with your financial planning, or with just your investments, is an A+ discussion. For the purposes of this book, I'm going to assume you're not at the point yet where you have to make that choice. Most Canadians never will be. That doesn't mean you can't eventually shift the load over to yourself; there's always that option if you are so inclined. But for now, I'm going to focus on what you should look for in financial advice.

(When you *are* ready for an A+ discussion on financial advisors, *The Professional Financial Advisor III* by John DeGoey is an outstanding book that I highly recommend.)

FINANCIAL PLANNING

You want a financial planner, or someone who actively offers financial planning as part of their services, as opposed to someone who only talks about investing.

But what is financial planning? Many people mistakenly believe that investing is financial planning, or vice versa. I know this from asking the uninitiated, "What do you think a financial planner does?" Very often the answer is, "I guess they help manage your investments." Generally speaking, there are a number of areas a comprehensive financial planner will look at, of which investing is only one. These areas are:

- insurance
- monthly budgeting
- debt management
- investing
- estate planning
- education planning
- retirement planning

Education and retirement planning involve investing, but belong in their own category, because you need to develop a plan that factors in how much you'll need for those goals, how much you have now, and how much you'll contribute along the way.

If you are going to be working with a financial advisor, you'll want to receive, and see samples of, a financial plan and an investment policy statement (IPS).

A Financial Plan

Creating a comprehensive financial plan is a semi-laborious process, but well worth the trouble. You start with a discovery meeting where the planner essentially asks you where you are and where you want to be. The first part includes figuring out your net worth (everything you own minus everything you owe), how much you earn, how much you spend, and your attitude towards money. It should also include gathering information about the insurance you have, and what your company benefits (if any) cover, and so on.

That first meeting might also include a discussion about where you ideally want to be at various points in the future. It will detail specific goals, such as paying for a wedding, whether you want to pay for your children's post-secondary education or not (or partially), saving up for a down payment on a house, how often you want to travel, and when you might like to retire (and what that retirement might look like).

After this discovery meeting, the planner will go away and start crunching numbers and analyzing different aspects of your finances. The planner might come back at a second meeting and provide a rough preliminary analysis that points out any holes in your current situation. Maybe you have kids, but no wills or insurance. Maybe you don't even run a surplus with your monthly cash flow. Maybe your current investments are too risky for you. He or she will also make recommendations about what your next steps should be. Certain insurance coverage, a less risky investment portfolio, saving more for retirement, or building up a larger emergency fund, are all potential topics for discussion. Once you've agreed on a financial plan that addresses all your concerns (and the planner's), you then need to execute and monitor the plan. The financial planner might be able to provide your insurance coverage, but you might get referred to a lawyer for your wills and powers of attorney.

Life happens all the time. You have another child, the stock market crashes, you have a big emergency expense, etc. Many variables affect the success of your financial planning, and a good financial planner will keep on top of them for you. Plan for an annual review, and a bigger meeting every few years, or as life circumstances dictate, and semi-regular contact over the phone or emails between meetings. You should always feel free to pick up the phone for any financial question you have, anytime.

Ideally, you'll end up with a written financial plan (one, moreover, that you fully understand) and an investment policy statement that speaks directly to your investment portfolios.

An Investment Policy Statement (IPS)

An investment policy statement is a document that outlines what your investment portfolio should look like, and how it will be adjusted over time. It allows you to make proactive, rather than reactive, decisions. Ideally, any transactions you make after having an IPS drawn up will require no thought: you just stick to the plan laid out in the IPS.

You would never get on a plane that hadn't settled on a destination ahead of time, so it boggles my mind to hear that so many people do not have an investment policy statement. It's almost the same scenario. And the same is true whether you are flying commercial (using an advisor), or are a pilot yourself (DIY). Few people invest purely as a hobby: their portfolios are a means to an end. With that in mind, it would seem prudent to have some kind of plan in place. If you are travelling towards a specific destination, it helps to look out the window every now and then, to make sure you are on track.

An IPS is specific to your investment portfolio, whereas a financial plan is more broadly encompassing (including estate planning, long-term tax planning, credit planning, cash flow, etc.). The IPS defines your tolerance for loss, what are acceptable and unacceptable investments for you, and what to do in response to different market events before they happen. It helps to take the emotional element out of investing.

Investment policy statements are similar to financial plans in that they can be simple or comprehensive. The benefit of using a financial advisor is that the good ones recognize what you need to see in order for you to be successful. For example, engineer clients tend to want a veritable tome of information that they can go through by themselves. These IPSs might include nuanced tests such as complex Monte Carlo sensitivity analyses (that can model hundreds of different sequences of portfolio returns) and can be more than 20 pages long. Present that to a non-engineer, or someone who has an aversion to graphs, and they'll prefer going to the dentist for a root canal.

Think of it this way: an IPS should be detailed enough that if your present advisor were to retire or pass away suddenly, your new advisor could pick up right where the last one left off. It has to be simple enough that it makes sense to you. You don't need to understand how the pilot flies the plane, but you certainly want to know if you're travelling to your destination, and how much turbulence to expect on the flight.

HOW MUCH DOES FINANCIAL ADVICE COST?

This is one of the many areas that can really obscure the subject. There are actually a few different ways to pay for financial advice, but let's break it down a little bit differently. You either see the fees and/or commissions you pay, or you don't. But you always pay fees or commissions. It's never free. Ever. Anyone who tells you otherwise should have their licence revoked.

When you don't see a line on any statement or transaction record regarding fees or commissions, that probably means they're built into the product. When you buy a life insurance policy, the commission can be greater than the first year's worth of premiums you pay. If you place a $100,000 order for a mutual fund, your advisor's firm might pocket $5,000 and give your advisor $4,000 from that, but you'll still see $100,000 on your statement.

How does this work?

First, it's worth pointing out that most Canadians invest in mutual funds when they start their investing career. A mutual fund is simply a turnkey portfolio that allows small investors to pool their money to get the benefits enjoyed by a large investor. Those benefits could include the ability to have a fully diversified portfolio, for example.

As a small investor, let's suppose you have only $100 per month to contribute to a portfolio. You might know that you don't want to hold all your eggs in one basket, and so you want to invest in different companies, different countries, some equities, some bonds, and so on. You want a diversified portfolio. With $100 per month, you can't really diversify on your own very quickly. But if instead you buy a unit of a mutual fund, you can own a share of a larger portfolio that is fully diversified. If the mutual fund goes up 10% in value, your share also goes up 10% in value.

Let me explain exactly how mutual funds make money for financial advisors in Canada.

HOW MUTUAL FUND SALES ARE COMPENSATED

In Canada, most mutual funds pay what are known as "trailers" to firms and advisors. It is a cost that can be embedded in the management expense ratio (MER) of a fund through the service fee. While there are a handful of mutual funds that do not charge a service fee (and resulting trailers), most of them do. (Note that F-Class funds represent versions of mutual funds that have the trailers stripped out of them, so that they can be held in special fee-based accounts where the service fees are charged separately.)

For the funds that do have service fees, there may be five different versions of the same fund: front-end load, back-end load, no-load, the newer low load (sometimes referred to as "level load"), and finally the F-class versions. Let's examine the differences by seeing how a representative sample fund can be sold under each option. Our sample fund is a Canadian equity mutual fund that has a management fee of 1.25% and other fees and expenses of 0.25% (brokerage costs, administration expenses, etc). Therefore, the mutual fund manufacturer's fee to operate this fund is 1.50%. The manufacturer is the company that actually picks the investments and runs the portfolio.

The manufacturer also adds a service fee. It is this service fee from which commissions are generated. The typical service fee is 1.00%, with a few exceptions as noted below. To make a long story short, the MER of this fund would be 2.50%, which is made up of the management fee and other operating expenses (1.50%) plus the service fee (1.00%).

Front-End Load Mutual Funds

A front-end load version of this mutual fund pays an ongoing trailer to the advisor of the typical 1%. This means the advisor will receive 1% of the average value of your investment in this fund over the course of every year. It is called a front-end load fund because the advisor additionally has the ability to charge you a front-end sales charge of between 0% and 5%, which gets deducted from your investment immediately. In many cases, fund companies will limit this to a maximum of 2% instead of 5%. (Further, many advisors will sell a front-end version of a fund with a front-end fee of 0%. They would do this when there is no specific no-load version of the same fund available and they would like the features associated with that version of fund.)

For example, if you invested $100,000 into a front-end load fund with a front-end load of 2%, your initial investment would be docked $2,000, which goes to the advisor, leaving $98,000 to be invested. Your advisor would earn a further 1% trailer per year of the amount in your account.

DSC Funds or Back-End Load Mutual Funds

Many funds are sold on a deferred sales charge, or declining sales charge (DSC) basis. This allows for the biggest upfront commission of any of the other versions (except for the advisor who would actually charge a 5% front-end load—which is pretty rare). It is important to note that DSC funds pay your advisor an upfront commission of 5%, even though this is not subtracted from your initial investment deposit. Rather, the fund manufacturer pays the advisor in advance for the future service fees that will be generated. The ongoing trailer fee to the advisor is reduced from 1% to 0.25% in exchange for the lump-sum, upfront commission.

It is also important to note that if you sell out of these funds, you are subject to a redemption fee for the first 7 years (plus or minus depending on the fund company). The redemption fee normally starts at 5% in the first year and then gradually declines to 0% after 7 years (which explains why these funds are sometimes referred to as "declining sales charge" funds). After the 7 years, there would be no fee charged to sell out of these funds.

This redemption fee is basically the fund company's assurance that the upfront commission to the advisor will be accounted for, should the investor sell out before the future service fees can be generated. Basically, if you sell out of your fund after year one, you pay a 5% penalty, which covers the fund company's initial commission to the advisor.

The service fee charged by the fund remains at 1%. The service fee shouldn't be confused with the trailer fee the advisor receives, which for DSC funds is 0.25%, as mentioned above. This means there is a 0.75% surplus the fund company is running every year and it is from this ongoing surplus that the upfront commission liability is paid off over the course of a little more than 6 years (hence, the 7-year redemption fee schedule).

If you invest $100,000 into a DSC fund, your advisor generates a $5,000 commission right away, and you still have $100,000 invested. The advisor additionally receives an ongoing trailer fee of 0.25% of the average value of your investment every year. If you sell out of your funds within the first 7 years, you are charged a redemption fee, which goes to the fund company to offset its upfront payment to the advisor.

Essentially, you are making a promise that you will stay invested for 7 years—or pay a penalty. Because the fund company has this guarantee from you, they can afford to pay a large lump sum to the advisor right away.

No-Load Funds

No-load funds have neither an initial front-end fee nor a DSC fee. In other words, you only have to worry about paying the ongoing MER for as long as you hold the fund. The advisor will generate a 1% commission every year based on the average value of your investment. They receive no upfront commission for no-load funds, just the ongoing trailer fee.

If you invest $100,000 in a no-load fund, you will have nothing deducted from your initial investment and your advisor will not earn an upfront commission, but they will still earn a 1% commission based on the average value of your investment every year. (In some very rare cases, a no-load fund may have a higher trailer than other versions of the same fund—which means it would have a higher service fee as well.)

Low-Load Funds

Just think of low-load (or level-load) funds as a scaled-back version of DSC funds, with a bit of a twist. The upfront commission is lower, averaging 3% versus the DSC's 5%. The redemption fees start at 3% and decline to 0% after 3 years, instead of the fees starting at 5% and declining to 0% after 7 years for DSC funds. But here is the twist: while the trailer fee is initially set to 0.25%, it increases to 1% as the redemption fee schedule expires. This is why it is also known as a "level-load" fund.

If you invest $100,000 into a low-load (or level-load) fund, you are not docked any money upfront. Your advisor receives $3,000 as an upfront commission and 0.25% of the average value of your account in the first year. He or she might receive 0.5% of the average value of your account in the second year, 0.75% in the third year, and then 1% every year thereafter.

F-Class Funds

The "F" stands for "fee" in fee-based account funds. These are a relatively new type of account, which charge clients a transparent fee that is easily seen on statements (where it's likely to be listed as the "client advisory fee"). This was introduced to address complaints made by investors who weren't sure what they were paying their advisors, because the compensation was essentially hidden or, at best, not transparently disclosed. For the F-class version of a fund there is *no* service fee. So, for our sample fund, that would mean that the MER has been reduced from the 2.50% in all the previous cases to 1.50%. *But* to make an apples-to-apples comparison, you need to add the client advisory fee to the MER to determine your all-in cost. While a fee-based account provides more transparency, it may not necessarily be cheaper. Typically, the client advisory fee for F-class funds is set to 1%: it is exactly the same as a no-load fund in terms of cost and flexibility (i.e., no charges to buy and sell), although a bit more transparent.

There is one important advantage of fee-based accounts for non-registered investment portfolios in that it is possible to claim the client advisory fee as a tax deduction on your tax return (you need to have your accountant verify this for your own situation to be sure). In this case, if your marginal tax rate was

40%, then the after-tax client advisory fee would be effectively 0.60% instead of 1%, meaning your out-of-pocket costs for an F-class version of a fund in a non-registered account would be 2.10% versus 2.50% for all the other fund versions.

If you invest $100,000 in an F-class mutual fund, your initial investment is not docked any upfront charge, and your advisor would not receive any upfront commission. The advisor would receive a percentage (typically 1%) of the average value of your account every year. There would be no cost to sell out of the F-class fund. For non-registered accounts, your client advisory fee may be tax-deductible (check with your accountant).

A final note: all the commissions noted here may not necessarily go to the advisor, but may instead be split between the advisor and the advisor's firm. Depending on the situation, the advisor normally receives between 40% and 80% of the commissions generated, although percentages below and above this range are also possible in certain situations.

DIFFERENT FEE MODELS

There are a number of pricing models for financial advice. Here are the major ones:

1. salary plus bonus
2. commission
3. fee-based
4. fee-for-service
5. a mix of models

You'll find salary-plus-bonus advisors at bank branches, for the most part. But the most prevalent model today is commission-based financial advice. These financial advisors earn a commission based on the type of product they sell you, whether it's mutual funds, stocks, insurance, or bonds. In the case of mutual fund sales, I've heard some people say they don't pay for advice. While they don't see a bill, they pay in the form of more expensive products, which have the cost of advice built into the product itself. If an advisor ever tells you that it doesn't cost you anything, run away as fast as you can. They are flat-out lying. They may rehearse a song-and-dance routine for your benefit about how someone else pays them, and it might sound convincing. But it's all smoke and mirrors.

Fee-based (for asset-based) advice is a growing trend in the industry. The fee is based on a percentage of your portfolio's value and is clearly shown on your financial statements. This model tries to separate the cost of advice from the cost of the product. You still pay, and it may not be cheaper, but it is more transparent.

A fee-for-service financial advisor might bill you

strictly by the hour, or by using a flat rate per project. They might charge $3,000 plus tax for a financial plan, for example. You might be free to buy the products on your own to implement the plan at self-serve costs and then head back for an annual review, for which you would also pay a fee. That $3,000 bill might be steep for a young client, but it could be a bargain when your portfolio is $1 million. A commission-based mutual fund sales representative might be costing you $10,000 per year in financial advice fees that are embedded in the products they've sold you.

Suffice it to say, it's a tricky discussion, considering you have to weigh various factors: the model of compensation, the size of your portfolio, and how much help you require. But don't over-think it (at least, not yet).

Here's what you need to know for now. No one works for free, and few people begrudge others for trying to earn an honest living. One of the first conversations to have with any prospective financial advisor is about the compensation they charge. Ask them exactly how they get paid, what conflicts of interest that exposes them to, and how their fee model compares to other models, and then shut up. Let them do all the talking. If they squirm, or are purposefully vague, tell them you don't expect them to work for free, and that they should just be candid. If they still seem shifty, run, don't walk, to another financial advisor.

I've found that one of the best determinants of a successful financial advisor is candour. Conflicts of interest are ubiquitous in life. The mere existence of a conflict of interest does not mean that advisors, or anyone else for that matter, are incapable of rising above them. But we have to recognize their existence, and recognize that there are some bad apples that really spoil the bunch.

When dealing with commissioned financial advisors, you have to understand that there is a strong correlation between how much they earn and how big your portfolio is. There is also a strong correlation between their *experience* and how big your portfolio is. That means that a larger percentage of experienced advisors might not take on a client with a small portfolio. Having said all this, you don't really need a comprehensive financial plan when you're just starting out.

The Five Rules are your plan for the time being. Once you've paid down all your high-interest debt, then you can start thinking about investing. (See Chapter 6 for a how-to guide.) When you are paying 28% interest on credit card debt, it doesn't make sense to invest when you would be lucky to see your money grow at even one-quarter of that rate.

When you first become an investor, the amount you invest is far more important than the makeup of your portfolio in determining how fast your portfolio grows. Remember the example from the introduction to this book? Two hundred dollars per month at 1.5% annual growth will give you almost $26,000 in 10 years. Put aside only $100 per month and to get the same portfolio value after 10 years you'll need more than 14% annual growth in your portfolio. How you set up your investments when you have a large portfolio is phenomenally important. How you set up your investments when you have a small portfolio is phenomenally *un*important. How much you contribute is what you need to focus on at first.

HOW TO PICK A FINANCIAL ADVISOR

Before you get too invested in a particular consultant, it pays to see if he or she is even registered as a financial advisor. Here are a number of steps you should take:

1. Check to see if they are registered as a financial advisor with the Canadian Securities Administrators through their National Registrant Search: www.securities-administrators.ca/nrs/nrsearch.aspx?id=850

2. If the advisor is *not* listed there, check with your provincial securities commission. Sometimes the information is not listed in both places.

You can call your securities commission and tell them you would like assistance confirming the registration of a financial advisor you are considering or are already doing business with.

- Alberta Securities Commission: 1-877-355-4488
- British Columbia Securities Commission: 1-800-373-6393
- Manitoba Securities Commission: 1-800-655-5244 (Toll-free within Manitoba only) or (204) 945-2548
- New Brunswick Securities Commission: 1-866-933-2222 (Toll-free within New Brunswick only) or (506) 658-3060
- Securities Commission of Newfoundland and Labrador: (709) 729-4189
- Northwest Territories Department of Justice: 1-867-920-3318
- Nova Scotia Securities Commission: (902) 424-2499
- Nunavut Registrar of Securities: (867) 975-6190
- Ontario Securities Commission: 1-877-785-1555
- Prince Edward Island Securities Office (PEISO), Office of the Attorney General: (902) 368-6288

- Quebec (Autorité des Marchés Financiers):
  1-877-525-0337
- Saskatchewan Financial Services
  Commission: (306) 787-5645
- Yukon Securities Office: (867) 667-5466

3. It's possible the advisor you are considering
   is not licensed as a financial advisor, but
   rather as an insurance agent. Check with your
   provincial regulator that handles life insurance
   agent registration.
   - Alberta Insurance Council: (403) 233-2929
     or (780) 421-4148
   - Insurance Council of British Columbia:
     1-877-688-0321
   - Manitoba Insurance Council: (204) 988-6800
   - New Brunswick, Department of Justice,
     Insurance Branch: (506) 453-2541
   - Newfoundland and Labrador: Try calling
     (709) 729-2595
   - Northwest Territories: (867) 920-8056
   - Nova Scotia, Office of the Superintendent of
     Insurance: (902) 424-5528
   - Nunavut, Superintendent: 1-867-873-7308
   - Financial Services Commission of Ontario:
     1-800-668-0128

- Prince Edward Island: 902-368-4937
- Quebec, Autorité des Marchés Financiers:
  1-877-525-0337
- Insurance Councils of Saskatchewan:
  (306) 347-0862
- Yukon: (867) 667-5940

4. You can also check to see if there have been
   any disciplinary actions taken against them:
   - www.iiroc.ca/English/Investors/MembInfo
     Service/DisciplinarySearch/Pages/default.
     aspx
   - www.mfda.ca/enforcement/hearingscurrent.
     html
   - www.mfda.ca/enforcement/hearingscomplete.
     html
   - www.mfda.ca/enforcement/hearingSchedule.
     html

   Check all four.

5. Google them to see what you dig up.

6. Ask them the following questions:
   - Are you a full-time financial advisor?
   - How do you get paid?
   - Do you use investment products
     manufactured by your own firm?

- How long have you been an advisor?
- Do you have a CFA, CFP, FCSI, or other relevant designation?
- Do you also sell life insurance?
- Do you have a sample investment policy statement I can look at?
- Do you have a sample financial plan I can look at?
- How many people are on your team?
- How often will we meet?

7. If they say they are a certified financial planner, you can also check their registration with the CFP licensing authority in Canada, Financial Planning Standards Council (FPSC), by calling 1-800-305-9886.

The specific answers you get are not as important as the advisor's demeanour. You should meet three or more different advisors before you decide on one to undertake your comprehensive financial plan. Keep in mind, if you are just starting out, generally you're going to end up with someone who might not tick off all the boxes, so to speak. But as your portfolio grows, your pickiness can grow too.

ADVISORS AND LIFE STAGES

Do you need a financial advisor when you are just starting out with your first investment portfolio? Or should you wait until you have achieved a certain asset level before working with a professional? These are somewhat leading questions that don't actually address the real question, which is, do you know what you don't know about managing personal finance?

Personal finance is about more than just rates of return, MERs, and diversification. These terms are meaningless if you haven't even made up your mind to start saving, because if you don't have a surplus, you've got nothing to invest. You can read Benjamin Graham and David Dodd's book, *Security Analysis*, until you've got it memorized, but without any skin in the game, it is all academic.

Perhaps the first thing a financial advisor will tell you is that you should stop your automatic contributions to a mutual fund portfolio and pay off your high-interest credit cards. Or perhaps you have five kids and no wills or powers of attorney: you know that's wrong, but you just need a gentle push to actually do something about it. A financial advisor may give you that push.

While there are some advisors who care only about your actual investment portfolio, they might be the ones who tend to work with very large portfolios (many millions of dollars) and with clients who have multiple advisors for different aspects of their financial affairs. But more and more, the average advisor provides advice, or access to advice, on all aspects of your financial situation.

Perhaps the question you really don't know you should be asking is whether you should change financial advisors over time based on your stage of life. One possible answer that may surprise you is: perhaps not, because they will change for you.

A change of advisors may come about for one of two main reasons. First, advisors are required continually to upgrade their education in order to maintain their registrations and designations. Products and legislation evolve all the time, and advisors are responsible for keeping up to date with both. They also gain experience as time goes on, obviously. Second, advisors may change firms or their type of registration. There are various reasons for this. Some firms' product platforms or planning support are better suited for certain advisors and their particular practice or philosophy. We're scratching the surface here, but suffice it to say, the advisor you started your investing career with can evolve as your portfolio and planning requirements evolve.

So if you're wondering when you should be looking for your first financial advisor, generally speaking, the average Canadian needs to start looking when they start dealing with money. Don't be shy about not having enough assets. Some advisors do have client minimums, but they'll often point you in the right direction based on your life-stage if you're not the right fit now.

DOES THE SIZE OF YOUR FINANCIAL PLAN MATTER?

It's not the size that matters: it's how you use it. I'm talking about financial plans. Everybody should have one, but one size does not fit all. That's true whether you are a DIY investor or are using a full-service advisor.

As the financial-advice industry continues to evolve, more and more advisors are offering comprehensive financial planning as part of their value proposition. Whether they have the CFP designation or not, many will have access to internal financial planning support teams, and some will even hire para-planners to prepare the financial plans on their behalf. Sometimes these plans can be more than 50 pages long. So should you feel like you're missing out if your plan is lacking in girth? Not necessarily.

If you are new to the workforce, what could you possibly expect to see in your financial plan that requires a document so long that the better part of a forest has to be sacrificed in its production? Unless you inherit a complex estate when you are young, more than likely you have all the same problems as everyone else: student debt, saving up for a mortgage, monthly budgeting, starting an investment plan, and getting the right type and amount of insurance to disaster-proof your life.

A plan written for a retirement date 40 years from now makes a lot of assumptions, many of which will turn out to be false, simply because no one knows what the future holds. Most people don't know ahead of time exactly how many children they will have—or even the number of their spouses.

When you're young, really, you just need to focus on putting away as much as you can, investing prudently, getting your debt under control, and hoping like mad that the stars align to allow you to retire earlier than you hoped. Retirement is so far off at this point that you'll have no idea what to expect, which means your buy-in to a 50-page plan is likely to be minimal. Many younger investors are better off with a plan that simply helps get them into good long-term habits while focusing on the shorter-term goals.

Fast-forward and, with diligence and luck, those habits will translate into an estate that needs an expert's advice. The range of possible outcomes to your life has narrowed and, as retirement approaches, it becomes much more top-of-mind. Your financial plan becomes more detailed, and hence thicker over time.

For DIY investors, the same thought process holds. You may have some rules to live by when you're starting out, but as time goes on you'll want to formalize your plan on paper. Especially as there is no guarantee you will outlive your spouse. That may be a case where size really does matter.

ARE YOU GETTING THE RUNAROUND?

Just because you hire an advisor to provide advice doesn't mean they are always right. Most people understand that recommendations are just that: recommendations. But when the advisor flat-out ignores you, you know you've got a big problem. So when I heard that good friends of mine were getting the runaround from their financial advisor and his company, my blood started to boil.

My friend, the investor, held shares of Nortel and was nervous about continuing to hold them. He asked his advisor to sell the shares if they fell below $34 in price. Although they fell in price, no shares were sold. The investor noticed the price had dropped below his target sell price while watching TV with his wife, who was in the hospital being treated for cancer. He didn't call his advisor immediately; he had other things on his mind.

He didn't find out until later that the shares were never sold. Naturally, he was upset and asked his advisor for an explanation. The advisor acknowledged the mistake, but persuaded the investor to hang on because analysts expected Nortel's share price to rise again. The investor reluctantly agreed, but with the stipulation that if the shares continued to fall and hit $30, they would be sold.

To make a long story short, the advisor never sold the shares. Nortel stock kept falling and the investor kept getting the runaround. For years. When the investor told me of these troubles, I suggested that he immediately make a complaint. I explained that the advisor's inaction constituted negligence.

Time passed but the firm did not conduct an investigation. Because there were no notes on file about my friend's instructions regarding Nortel, and because the advisor had now changed his story and denied ever having discussed selling the stock, the firm sided with the advisor. The investor never heard from the advisor again and the branch manager was assigned to take over the account.

My friend is following up through a second-stage complaint procedure with the Ombudsman for Banking Services and Investments (OBSI), but even if they rule in his favour, there is some question as to whether or not the decision would have any impact. The case is difficult to assess because there was no transaction (which is the point) and there are no notes about either selling or holding Nortel in the advisor's client file. So it has become a he-said-she-said situation.

Financial advisors are supposed to document every material discussion they have with an investor. Usually they are urged to do so from internal compliance officers who want to make sure that when, not if, they eventually get a complaint, there is documentation to support the actions that were taken. If disputes are investigated, one of the things looked at is the consistency of the advisor's notes. Some are more scrupulous than others about documenting their actions, and the ones who regularly attach notes to client files in a timely manner are going to stand a better chance under scrutiny than the ones who don't.

But there is something investors can do to help their cause: they can make their own notes. The Canadian Securities Administrators provide a handy worksheet* you can download for free to help you make notes on any conversation you have had with your advisor. You

---

* Google: "When your broker calls, take notes," and select the Canadian link for the PDF file.

should note any material discussions you have, and date and store them with your other records. Investor disputes are tough cases to win in Canada, but with lots of money on the line, it pays to take the time to make your own notes. It may not make the fight more even, but it's certainly better than doing nothing.

You hire an advisor to give you advice, but it's ultimately you who makes the decisions. Not the advisor.

A MONEY COACH INSTEAD OF A FINANCIAL ADVISOR

One of the Catch-22s of the financial-advice industry in Canada is that sometimes you find motivated individuals who desperately want to work with a financial advisor, but it might not make sense from a revenue perspective for that advisor to take them on as a client. A money coach might be worth considering for people in this situation.

Not all, but many financial advisors set minimum asset requirements for prospective clients. Don't have $1 million? Go see someone else. Some advisor teams have asset minimums of $10 million or more, and some set the bar as low as $50,000. There are also those who have no minimum at all. As you can imagine, because the bulk of advisors' revenues is closely tied to the assets they manage, there is a trade-off between the number of their clients and the amount of work they perform for each one.

If you have a large estate, you are going to gravitate towards an advisory team that specializes in larger estates. They will have fewer clients but should, in theory, be spending more time crafting a plan for your more complex situation. If you are just starting out, you might find yourself working with an advisor who handles many more clients but their investment policy statements and financial plans are much less onerous. So they can meet your needs, as well as the needs of hundreds of other people in a similar situation.

I haven't performed any double-blind studies to the effect, but based on what I've seen in the industry, advisory team experience and knowledge are pretty strongly correlated with the portfolio size of their average client. In other words, the more money you have, the better advisor you might have access to. Nothing earth-shattering about that. Rightly or wrongly, however, the desire to work with tested advisors leads many people to avoid newer advisors who are precisely the ones most likely to take them on as clients.

One solution to this conundrum is the idea of working with a money coach, that is, someone who coaches you on money decisions. I liken it to personal finance therapy.

You know by now that I believe that basic personal financial success boils down to the Five Rules (see Part 1). It's not rocket science, and yet many people have difficulty with some of these ideas. In fact, before you can work with a financial advisor who will handle your assets and create a detailed financial plan, you first have to generate those assets. And, generally there won't be significant assets unless you've got at least a partial handle on most of the core competencies described in my rules. This is where a money coach may be just the ticket.

They generally work on a flat fee or hourly basis. Most get no compensation for recommending particular products. You can expect a range between $1,000 and $2,000 for a basic coaching package.

I've heard of some financial advisors who send their clients to money coaches—a testament to how the work they perform is different from the services offered by a traditional financial advisor. Many financial advisors offer money coaching as part of their service offering too, so make sure to ask your advisor about it. In the future, I can see financial advisors and money coaches working in tandem as they can perform very different functions—both of which can be integral to your long-term financial success.

CHAPTER EIGHT

INSURANCE 101

This is the lengthiest section in the book, but once we get through it, you'll probably look at life insurance much differently. To start, we have to get a basic understanding of the machine that is life insurance. An insurance expert shared a story with me that quickly brought me up to speed on the basics when I was training to get my licence. While it's been some time, allow me to recount the gist of that story ...

Let's go back a few hundred years. Lloyd, a wealthy man, was a frequent visitor to a certain pub. Now, Lloyd was always looking for ways to make more money. Everyone in town knew of Lloyd's wealth and they would come to the pub to ask for his money for business transactions, for loans, or just to plain beg.

One day, a farmer came to Lloyd and said, "Listen, I have a problem. It's July and my crops are due to be harvested in August. We've had a fantastic year and we'll earn more selling this year's crops than for the last 5 years combined."

Lloyd retorted, "That hardly sounds like a problem, friend!"

"Well," continued the farmer, "hear me out. I am the only one in the household who can harvest those crops—without me, the crops will sit and die and become worthless. I know that once I harvest those crops I can stop working for life. But I am close to 40 years old [which was really old back then] and I would like to make sure that no matter what happens to me, my family will be taken care of. Even if it costs me money for that peace of mind."

Lloyd thought for a moment. And then he said to the farmer, "Here's what I can offer you. I want you to give me 20 gold coins right now. If you die in a month's time, before the harvest has been gathered, I will give your family 100 gold coins. Of course, if you don't die, I get to keep your 20 coins. What do you say to that?"

Lloyd had done some fast thinking before he made his offer. This farmer appeared to him to be in exceptionally good health for a 40-year-old. Lloyd knew that for every one hundred 40-year-old men in town, on average, five would die in the next month. Lloyd was willing to bet that this farmer wouldn't be one of them.

The farmer agreed to this scheme—and he survived to harvest and sell his last crop. He retired wealthy, so the story has a happy ending. Lloyd was happy too: he had 20 gold coins that he did not have before making his "bet" on the farmer's life.

So much for my story. Now let's take a look at the math.

The statistical odds of that farmer dying were 5 in 100 (or 1 in 20), which is a 5% chance. So there was a 5% chance that Lloyd would lose his bet on the farmer's life and have to pay out the 100 gold coins. Bearing in mind that he had collected 20 gold coins from the farmer, he would really only be out 80 gold coins. So from Lloyd's point of view, there was a 95% chance that he would make 20 gold coins versus a 5% chance that he would lose 80 gold coins. He was wealthy enough to come up with the 80 coins if necessary, so he decided to take the risk.

But Lloyd *was* taking a risk: it was possible that the farmer would've died. So, instead of just charging the farmer 5 gold coins (which would be the statistical break-even point), he charged more (20 gold coins). He did this to compensate for the risk he was taking.

Let's fast-forward 10 years. Lloyd's scheme caught on like wildfire and other people were coming up to Lloyd with the same, or a very similar, proposition: they wanted to be insured for 100 gold coins in exchange for a fee to be set by Lloyd. Lloyd was shrewd enough to know that if he lowered the fee (or, to give it its familiar name, the premium), he would attract more customers. As he attracted more customers, he could lower the premiums. He knew that one bad bet wouldn't wipe him out because there would be 20 good bets for each bad one. He knew this because he had studied the population statistics of his town.

So let's look at this new business Lloyd has set up for himself. This year, 1,000 men (all aged 40) have bought a life insurance policy from him for the next month. He knows that statistically 50 of those men will die and he will have to pay out 5,000 gold coins (50 men × 100 gold coins) in death benefits. He also knows that 950 men will survive. If he wants just to break even, he has to generate 5,000 gold coins in premiums from all 1,000 men, so he could charge them each just 5 gold coins instead of 20.

But being the businessman that he is, Lloyd knows that some months 60 of 1,000 men will die, and some months 40 of 1,000 men will die. He doesn't want to get caught out. In exchange for the risk he is taking, and to make sure that his time isn't being wasted (this new endeavour is now taking up all his time), he charges an extra 2 gold coins on top of the 5 needed to break even—and to make sure that he makes a profit. So during the next month, he collects 7 gold coins each from 1,000 men (a total of 7,000 gold coins) and pays out 5,000 gold coins. He now is earning an average 2,000 gold coins per month.

Now let's look at this from the insured person (or policyholder's) point of view. They also know that 50 out of 1,000 men like them will die in the next month. By taking out the policy and paying the 7 gold coins, they win—in a manner of speaking—if they die: their family receives 100 gold coins in exchange for 7. It is a morbid way to think about insurance, I know. The insurance company wins if you don't die, because they keep your premium and don't pay out a death benefit.

TERM LIFE INSURANCE

Now we are ready to build on some simple concepts. Let's talk about how premiums rise as you get older. Once we understand this, we will have a lot of the groundwork covered.

Remember how the statistics for a 40-year-old man, way back when, indicated that he had a 5-in-100 chance of dying in the next month? Well, let's fast-forward a little bit. Let's say that a 40-year-old man (due to improvements in health care and quality of life) now has a 5-in-100 chance of dying within the next *year*. As you know, your chances of dying go up with age. So, statistically, a 41-year-old man has a slightly higher mortality rate than the 40-year-old, and a 39-year-old would have a slightly lower mortality rate than the 40-year-old.

But let's take a closer look. Maybe the 39-year-old has a 4-in-100 chance of dying (4%), while the 40-year-old's chances of dying remain 5 in 100 (5%). The 41-year-old might have a 7-in-100 chance (7%). In this case, the *amount of change* between the 39-year-old and the 40-year-old's chance of dying is less than the *amount of change* between the 40-year-old and the 41-year-old's chance of dying.

Another way to explain this is that, all else being equal, you would expect that a 25-year-old in average health has little chance of dying in the next year, while a 99-year-old in average health has a pretty good chance of dying in the next year. As you get older, your chances of dying increase exponentially. The 99-year-old's chances of dying might be 95 in 100.

The general trend of mortality can be directly translated into insurance premiums. The higher your chance of dying, the higher your premium will be. So in Figure 8.1, you can consider the Y axis as either mortality or the insurance premium amount.

The graph shows how insurance premiums increase exponentially as a function of age. From this we can extrapolate that if someone were to apply for an insurance policy every year, the cost in each successive

Figure 8.1: Mortality and insurance premiums

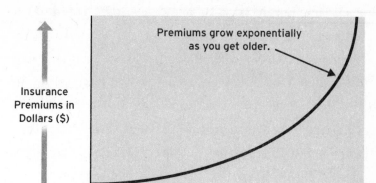

Insurance Premiums in Dollars ($)

Premiums grow exponentially as you get older.

Age

year would increase, until at some point it becomes unaffordable.

For someone very young, the premiums are relatively inexpensive. I remember a client aged 26 or so requesting a $250,000 life insurance policy whose premiums were around $130 per year. For someone very old, the annual premium on a policy for the same amount will actually approach $250,000 per year: the premium and potential payout are virtually the same. Of course, at this point it becomes pointless to purchase the insurance, because it would be silly to pay $250,000 for the year if you collect only $250,000 if you die.

Let's break it down a little further. For a 25-year-old, we know the premiums are fairly cheap. If this person could spread out the cost of the insurance over a set time period (say, 10 years), he or she could pay a set yearly or monthly amount for the entire 10 years. Why would they do this? Well, the set payment will be higher than the amount they would have to pay in the first of the 10 years, and lower in the last of the 10 years, so they are averaging it out. The idea is that they are willing to pay a little bit more than they should early on, so that they can pay less than they need to later in the term. This way they keep the cost of insurance affordable as they get older.

Now look at Figure 8.2: we have inserted vertical lines at 10-year intervals. In the beginning, the growth rate in annual premiums is relatively small, but as the person gets older and the premiums increase exponentially, you can see why choosing a longer term becomes desirable. Insurance coverage becomes more desirable as you get older because people realize they have a greater chance of dying as they get older, which is exactly when the costs are greater.

Now we understand the basis of term life insurance. There are different lengths of term available: the most popular are 10- and 20-year terms. (There is also term-to-100, which is a bit of an anomaly, so we will cover that later.) Term life insurance is known as temporary insurance because there comes a point at which it is unaffordable (when you are really old). When you are

Figure 8.2: Term life insurance evens out the cost of premiums

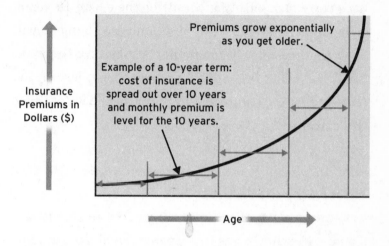

Premiums grow exponentially as you get older.

Example of a 10-year term: cost of insurance is spread out over 10 years and monthly premium is level for the 10 years.

Insurance Premiums in Dollars ($)

Age

younger, however, it is quite cheap and affordable. It stays in effect for as long as you pay your premiums—if you miss a month, your policy gets cancelled and you get no money back. (There is a provision to pay your late premium owing within a certain period of time to allow for your policy not to lapse.)

Term life is most often needed for temporary insurance needs. One example of this is to cover your mortgage: you want the mortgage paid off if you die, so you get insurance to cover the balance. Of course, the balance goes down over time and, all things being equal, one day you are mortgage-free, so the need for mortgage insurance is temporary.

Okay, so the take-home message of this section is that term life is temporary insurance, and for the better part of your life, it will be the cheapest form of insurance coverage you can get. As you get older, however, term life will eventually become unaffordable. Next, we will take a look at permanent insurance. (Whole life and universal life insurance also fall into this category.)

WHOLE LIFE INSURANCE

Let's start with the basics of whole life insurance. There are certain costs that people would like paid for when they die, but if they are older we know that term life insurance is too expensive. Many companies will not even offer term life once you are around 80. But, of course, even 80-year-olds have some life insurance requirements, namely: funeral costs (if they don't want to burden their loved ones); inheritances (if they want to make a larger estate available to their heirs); taxes (if they have a large tax liability when they die, they may want to have enough insurance to pay the tax bill).

One of the top reasons cottages go for sale in Muskoka (one of Canada's most popular recreation areas) is that the owner has died and the next generation can't afford the tax bill. The only way to pay it is to sell the property.

The solution for these permanent insurance needs is whole life insurance (which is a type of permanent insurance; universal life, which we will cover later, is the other form of permanent insurance). Whole life insurance never expires (as long as you keep paying your premiums) and the premiums never increase. It is much more expensive at first than term life, because you are averaging the cost of insurance over your entire life (as opposed to averaging it out for a limited term of, for example, 10 years), but while it is much more expensive when you are younger, it looks like a real bargain when you are older. Figure 8.3 provides a visual idea of how this works.

Figure 8.3: Whole life insurance becomes a bargain in later life

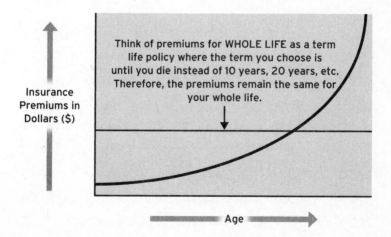

Insurance Premiums in Dollars ($)

Think of premiums for WHOLE LIFE as a term life policy where the term you choose is until you die instead of 10 years, 20 years, etc. Therefore, the premiums remain the same for your whole life.

Age

When you take whole life insurance, you overpay the cost when you are younger in order to be able to afford it when you most need it—when you are very old. There are a few more ideas we need to discuss in relation to whole life before we get to universal life—in fact, this is where it starts to really get interesting.

Let's now look at what the insurance companies do with the overpayment in the early years of a whole life insurance policy. We know the monthly premiums in the early years of a whole life insurance policy are much higher than the pure cost of insurance, which is the curved line that increases exponentially with age (see Figure 8.4). People agree to overpay in the early years

Figure 8.4: Premium overpayments and underpayments offset each other over time

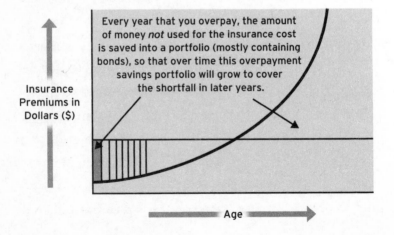

Insurance Premiums in Dollars ($)

Every year that you overpay, the amount of money *not* used for the insurance cost is saved into a portfolio (mostly containing bonds), so that over time this overpayment savings portfolio will grow to cover the shortfall in later years.

Age

because this makes it possible for them to afford the premiums later on in life. (Note how the pure cost of insurance indicates the premiums become unaffordable as you get very old.)

But what does the insurance company do with the overpayments? As you can imagine, they don't just put it under the mattress. They take the money and purchase a bond portfolio (with some stocks and other investments). Usually the bonds are very long term and very solid (e.g., 30-year government bonds). They invest conservatively because these insurance policies are going to be in place for a long time in most cases, and they need to make sure that they have the money to pay the claims. The proportion of stocks, short-term bonds, and bonds of lower credit quality in their portfolios are kept to a minimum.

Now, let's look at what happened with whole life policies in the 1980s, which caused a lot of change in the life insurance industry. (I'll give you a hint: the insurance companies made a lot of money on the bonds and ended up making huge profits.) If you look again at Figure 8.4, you can see that the overpayments go into an overpayments savings portfolio. This investment portion of the whole life policy grows over time, as the investments and the ongoing contributions increase this pool of funds.

The high interest rates of the 1980s created lots

of change in the types of insurance that companies offered. So the first thing you might be thinking is, what do interest rates have to do with insurance policies?

If you remember, the overpayment in the early years is directed into an investment portfolio that is predominantly fixed-income in nature. The rate of return on fixed-income investments is closely tied to prevailing interest rates. During the 1980s, interest rates were incredibly high—around 20% at the peak. When insurance companies are figuring out the insurance premiums for whole life, they first factor in the expected death of the life-insured individual along with that person's current age. This allows them to calculate how much the pure cost of insurance is. If, for example, you are expected to die at 85, are 25 now, and would like $500,000 in coverage, they will calculate how much money they will need from you over the next 60 years so that they will have $500,000 to give you when you're 85. If you live longer, you lose in the sense that you overpaid for the $500,000. If you die early, you win. They also factor in how fast they can make the money you give them grow.

So with whole life, where you are overpaying in the early years, the insurance company's investment portfolio's rate of return needs to be estimated for a very long period of time because once the premium has been determined, the insurance company is stuck with it. And, of course, because the insurance companies are meant to be profitable, they will tack on an additional amount to cover their expenses and to produce a profit for their services. Because of this, they tend to underestimate the rate of return on their investment portfolios when calculating premiums, which means premiums go up in price.

Well, during the 1980s, and specifically after interest rates had started to come back down, the insurance companies were being a little too cautious with their estimates. Whereas the premiums were based on perhaps a 6% long-term rate of return, they were collecting 10% or more on their investment portfolios. So let's say in any given year that 100 people with policies died, and they all had policies for $500,000. The insurance company was on the hook for $50 million. But they knew that, and using the estimated rate of return for the portfolios (6%) they would have set aside $60 million—enough to pay the claims with something left over for expenses and profit. But since the portfolios grew at 10%, maybe they actually had $120 million, so they had $70 million left over after paying the $50 million in death benefits.

Check the price histories of insurance companies during this period: they were among the best stocks to own because they were money-making machines. So what happened after that? Well, people became wise to their extraordinary profitability and they decided to do something about it.

Let's now look at the change spawned by infuriated policyholders (infuriated, that is, by the amount of money the insurance companies were making on the investment pools inside whole life policies). People started to "buy term and invest the rest." That is to say, they would buy term life insurance, paying premiums closer to the pure cost of insurance and much cheaper than the premiums for whole life insurance, and then they would take the amount that would have gone to the whole life premium (less the term insurance premium) and invest it themselves. The underlying rationale for this strategy was that the invested savings would grow at rates that were available in the market (the same rates the insurance companies were enjoying) and it would grow enough so that individuals would become effectively self-insured as they grew older. They would still have the coverage early on through the term policy, but would later shed their insurance coverage (and premiums) as the investment pool grew large enough to cover their needs.

Of course, big companies pay attention only to the language spoken by consumers' wallets. So "participating whole life" became more popular. "Participating" in this context meant that the policyholders would participate in the performance of the investment pool. If the investment pool grew faster than predicted, then the policyholders would get the extra growth returned to them in a number of different forms. On the flip side, if the investment pool underperformed, the policyholders would not be held accountable for making up the shortfall. This participation of the policyholders in the actual performance of the investment portfolio made whole life insurance more popular again.

Whole life insurance policies (which are a form of permanent insurance) are used for expenses that you incur only when you die, that can't be avoided no matter when you die. I realize this sounds like a minor point, but let's look at an example of when you wouldn't need a permanent insurance solution.

A lot of people buy insurance to cover the mortgage balance, reasoning that if one of the breadwinners dies, the surviving family members will not have to change their lifestyle drastically because of strained financial circumstances. But you might not have a mortgage balance when you die—especially if you live to be 80 or so. Chances are you will have paid it off by then. So this is a perfect example of a temporary insurance need. On the flip side, costs for a funeral can be huge, and sometimes people don't have the thousands of dollars with which to pay for these costs when they die. This is an example of a cost that necessarily happens only when you die, and therefore is a permanent need. While the costs of whole life insurance are greater than for term life, permanent insurance needs tend to be lower than temporary needs.

When you are younger, you may find that you need more insurance coverage than later on. This is because you have few assets coupled with large obligations. These may include the mortgage and an income for your young family to live on if you are not there to provide it yourself. In this case, you see term policies with coverage in the $1-million range on a regular basis (whereas a whole life policy might be in the $25,000–$50,000 range for an average person). The $1 million policy might cover a $250,000-mortgage balance and the remaining $750,000 could pay for your income replacement for 15 years.

While the amount of term life might be highest when you are starting your family, the cost is still fairly affordable because you are less likely to die when you are young. As you start saving and paying down the mortgage, you increase your net worth and decrease your need for insurance because in your absence your family can use the saved-up assets.

As shown in Figure 8.5, when you die, and if you are lucky enough to live to an old age, you may have sufficiently substantial assets to forgo the need for insurance altogether (assuming you were a good

**Figure 8.5: As your assets accumulate,
your need for term insurance declines.**

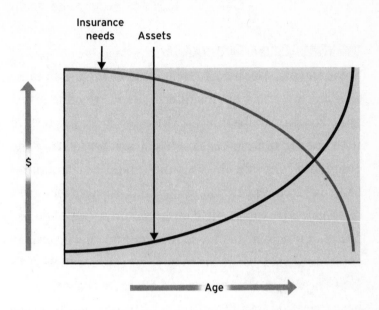

saver). In fact, many people do not need any type of insurance—even whole life—when they get older. I mentioned earlier that one possible use for whole life insurance is to pay terminal taxes. Some people believe that there is no need to cover the tax liabilities faced by their heirs: this is purely a personal choice. Am I advocating that you shouldn't have insurance of any kind when you get older? Of course not. What I'm saying is that you need to analyze your needs and your personal beliefs on money management and inheritances, and then make up your own mind.

UNIVERSAL LIFE INSURANCE

Some people, looking at the relatively high premiums charged for whole life insurance, asked why the insurance companies were not a little bit more aggressive with their investment selections. They figured that the companies' investment accounts could be structured to grow more quickly and so fund more of the cost of the policy, which ultimately would mean that the premiums would go down. Of course, the insurance companies had to make sure they could weather all types of market conditions and a largely fixed income-based portfolio was the best way to do this. In other words, the insurance companies didn't want to have to deal with investment accounts that didn't grow enough to fund the premium underpayment in later years.

Because the insurance companies didn't want to take on the risk of an aggressively managed portfolio performing poorly, they created the universal life insurance product. This allowed the policyholder to determine how the investments were structured. If they performed well, it benefited the policyholder. If they performed poorly, the policyholder would be on the hook for the shortfall. The term "universal" came about because you can structure this type of insurance to behave like any other type of life insurance product, if you know what you are doing.

So, as illustrated in Figure 8.6, the insurance company has granted the policyholder the ability to select the investments that go into the investment component in exchange for being responsible for the account's performance. Many policyholders believed this to be a fair arrangement, and universal life became

Figure 8.6: Universal life insurance gives the policyholder discretion to direct the investments inside the policy

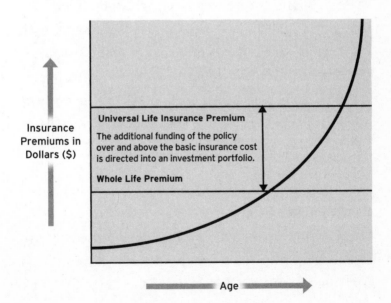

attractive, especially to those who had an insurance need and some market savvy. Up to certain limits, the policyholder can also "overfund" a universal life policy by adding even more money into the investment portfolio than is required just to keep the policy in force. One reason people do this is because this investment account has some tax-sheltering advantages.

To reiterate, a universal life insurance policy is similar to a whole life insurance policy in that there is an insurance component *and* an investment component. On the one hand, with whole life the goal of the investment component is to lower the cost of insurance over the course of the policyholder's lifetime by taking the overpayments early on and investing them, eventually growing them enough to pay for the underpayment later on. On the other hand, with universal life the policyholder has the ability to adjust the amount of the overpayment, and also to direct the actual investment allocation of the investment account. There are numerous reasons and strategies for this flexibility.

CALCULATING RISK

Okay, so how much life insurance do you need? I have come across way too many people who have no idea why they have as much insurance as they do. Their explanations range from, "my father told me to get this amount," and "it sounded like a good number," to "I really don't know." I find that very few people really know why they bought what they bought, and more importantly, how to adjust the amount as time goes on.

A good place to start is with a ballpark figure based on a simple set of calculations. Trust me, they *are* simple. Once you understand the basic philosophy behind the ballpark calculation, you can incorporate the details to match your own situation and preferences. Many calculations will vary based on your personal preferences, as you will see.

First, we need to realize that we have two types of needs: *immediate* cash requirements, and *ongoing* cash requirements.

Immediate Cash Requirements

These are expenses that are incurred upon the death of a spouse. For example, one requirement is to have the mortgage and other debts (such as an outstanding credit card balance) paid off. A funeral would also be an immediate expense. The insured person also may want to make sure the children's educations are paid for and have a lump sum added to the immediate requirements for this purpose. He or she may also want the surviving spouse to be able to take 6 months off work for bereavement. All of these needs and desires need to be added up.

Ongoing Cash Requirements

Normally, both spouses will have estimated how much household income will be required to maintain their lifestyle if one of them dies. A quick method would be to take the total current household income and multiply by 75%. So if one person makes $100,000 and the other makes $50,000 (for a total of $150,000), then 75% of their combined income ($112,500) would be required to maintain the family's lifestyle after the death of one spouse. You can also calculate the exact number by subtracting certain expenses that disappear when that spouse dies (e.g., vehicle payments for their car, clothing for work, meals, hobbies, etc.), if you want to be more accurate. But there may be certain items you've gotten used to (e.g., vacation with the kids to Disneyland every year) that you want to maintain, and this, coupled with other expenses, may be too much for one income. Depending on whether the surviving spouse wants to work or focus on raising the kids, or whether he or she was the breadwinner, this amount needed for ongoing household income can vary quite a bit.

So now we have talked about immediate and ongoing needs. Next we need to subtract what you already have in terms of assets and estimate the surviving income to find out what the shortfall is. You purchase insurance for the shortfall—not the total amount you require. An easy way to sort all of this out is illustrated in Figure 8.7.

If you read across the top two boxes as if they were a math equation, you take the immediate needs at death and subtract the immediate resources at death. These resources include current insurance (e.g., insurance coverage through your work benefits), savings that you would be willing to use (this may or may not include RRSPs), etc. In the example illustrated in the figure, we see that the current assets and insurance do not

Figure 8.7: A simple way to calculate the amount of life insurance you need.

Intermediate Needs at Death:		Intermediate Resources at Death:	
Mortgage	$150,000	Life insurance through work	$150,000
Loans and debts	$25,000		
Final expenses	$25,000	Savings (not including RRSP)	$25,000
Education fund	$80,000		
	$280,000		**$175,000**

Ongoing Income Requirement for Family:	Ongoing Income of Surviving Spouse:
$50,000	$30,000

quite cover the immediate needs at death—there is a $105,000 shortfall.

The bottom two boxes compare the ongoing family income requirement and the survivor's ongoing income. In this case, the family has decided that once the mortgage and other debts are paid off and the children's education funds are accounted for, then they don't require an extravagant amount of money to keep the surviving family members' standard of living intact. Further, in this case the surviving spouse would like to keep working (perhaps the children are old enough to not need supervision during the day). After we subtract the ongoing family income after death from the ongoing family income requirement, there is a small shortfall of $20,000 per year.

The key to that last sentence is in the phrase "per year." Twenty thousand dollars in life insurance today will cover the deficit for only 1 year, and naturally the surviving spouse may need to cover that shortfall for many years. Let's assume now that the surviving partner requires that support for 18 years, until the kids have moved out of the house. At that point, the survivor can live on one income. There are numerous ways to provide for this shortfall, and again it comes down to personal preference, but let's walk through the options.

The simplest method is to multiply $20,000 by

18 years. (We won't worry about inflation or the potential growth of the lump-sum insurance payment.) In this case, $20,000 × 18 years = $360,000. Add that to the $105,000 in immediate needs at death and the required coverage is $465,000. After 18 years, there would be no more insurance money, but presumably the surviving spouse would no longer have children at home, potentially has found a new partner, etc.

Another option is known as the "capital retention method." In this case, you calculate how much of a lump sum invested each year at a conservative rate of return would produce $20,000 per year in interest after tax. Working backwards: $20,000 after tax is equal to $28,500 before tax (assuming roughly 30% marginal tax rate). Suppose the lump sum is invested conservatively in government bonds at an annual growth rate of 5%.* The desired yield of $28,500 would be produced by a lump sum of $570,000. If you add this to $105,000, you have a total coverage requirement of $675,000. The point to note is that the beneficiary will always have the $570,000 lump sum. Many people like this method precisely because it provides for a retirement nest egg for the surviving spouse as well as providing an ongoing income until that point.

---

* 5% for a conservative government bond is quite a bit higher than current rates, so make sure to use current rates in your analysis.

The last main method is the "capital depletion method." This means that eventually the lump sum will decrease to zero, as it would be used to fund the annual costs. In this case, you would encroach upon the capital so that each year the $20,000 required cash flow would be funded by the interest earned on the lump sum *plus* the yield realized by selling off part of the lump sum itself. Eventually, at the end of 18 years, the lump sum will have been depleted to zero. Using my trusty calculator, I can tell you that you would need a lump sum of roughly $280,000 invested at 5%, assuming a marginal tax rate of 30%, to provide $20,000 in after-tax income for 18 years. Doing the math: $280,000 + $105,000 = $385,000, which is the total insurance required. Again, at the end of 18 years, you would have no insurance money left.

Note that I have not included the math for factoring in inflation. You can do this easily by subtracting the inflation estimate from the rate of return estimate. For example, if you think inflation will run at 3%, and you think you can get 5% on your conservative investment, then you would use 2% as the *real* rate of return on your lump sum investment. By dividing by a smaller number you get a larger answer (i.e., a larger lump sum) that will account for inflation. Suffice it to say, when factoring in inflation for the capital depletion method, the lump sum amount increases from $280,000 to about $370,000.

A couple more points to finish off and then we're done. Which of the three methods we've discussed is the best? Perhaps the best way to figure that out is to calculate the premium costs of each. For a 30-year-old male non-smoker:

- $465,000 Term 10 would cost $29.86 per month (18 years × $20,000 + $105,000)
- $675,000 Term 10 would cost $37.25 per month (capital retention method: lump sum invested, no depletion of principal)
- $385,000 Term 10 would cost $25.60 per month (capital depletion method: lump sum invested *with* depletion of principal)

Personally, I would choose the capital depletion method. It will be the cheaper option, while still providing the proper amount of insurance and it doesn't give your spouse *that* much of an incentive to kill you. But it's all up to your personal preferences.

The last significant calculation is to determine how much goes into term insurance and how much into whole life. Normally, you would match the need to the product (as they say). Term is a temporary solution. Whole life is a permanent solution. The only permanent needs are the need for funeral expenses and perhaps taxes and estate equalization. All the other expenses generally approach zero as you get older (mortgage gets paid off, kids leave home, spouse retires, etc.). But no matter what, there is always a funeral to be paid for. For this, you could consider a whole life policy to cover funeral expenses (say, for example, $15,000) and term for the rest.

Generally, it makes more sense to get the shorter terms (5 or 10 years) because, as you get older, acquire more assets, and pay off debts and mortgages, your need for insurance goes down. You can always adjust the coverage you have downwards by filling out a form, and therefore reducing your costs over time.

It's important to use an insurance broker who can compare quotes at many companies. It's not unusual to see a 10-year-term product offered at a cheaper rate than a competitor's 5-year term. But beyond that, this chapter has been a lot of information to take in. A good advisor can help you run through your own insurance needs analysis in case anything is unclear.

EPILOGUE

Well, that's it. We've reached the end. For some reason I always get a bid sad when I get to the end of a book. Parting is such sweet sorrow. But let's review what we tried to achieve together.

The fundamentals of financial success are easily understood but hard to implement. Set aside some time to reflect on what you want to achieve with your personal finances. You now know the financial equivalents of eating healthy and how to do a sit-up (and all the other basic exercises). It's up to you to put it all into action. You have the formula for an easy A. And for those of you who are ready, or who soon will be ready, you can start your journey for the harder-fought A+.

And I'm happy to provide some guidance along the way. Please don't hesitate to reach out on Twitter. You can find me at @preetbanerjee. I look forward to hearing from you!

INDEX